The 9 Gifts of The HOLY SPIRIT

God's Expression of Himself Through You

The 9 Gifts of The HOLY SPIRIT

God's Expression of Himself Through You

Christopher Lynn

The 9 Gifts *of* The HOLY SPIRIT

God's Expression of Himself Through You

First Edition

First Printing 2019

ISBN: 978-0-578-21262-3

GLORIOUS FAITH PUBLICATIONS, INC.

"Seeing the Unseen, Hearing the Unheard,

Speaking the Spoken Word"

Christopher Lynn Ministries, Inc.

PO Box 521072 Tulsa, OK 74152

For more information call 918-895-4136

Visit us online at www.gloriousfaith.org

Edits by: Brooke Delong, Linda Noble and Christopher Lynn

Cover Design by: Cassidy Cagle

For Worldwide Distribution, Printed in the U.S.A

Dedication

To all the Men and Women of God who paved the way upon which we now tread.

"Of whom the world was not worthy." ***Hebrews 11:38***

Table of Contents

INTRODUCTION

At the age of 14 my life was forever changed in a moment...
Even as a young child, I had a deep sense of destiny. I always seemed to
feel there was a greater purpose for my life than just existing. I grew up
in Church like a lot of people, but also like them, I had never really
understood what knowing Christ was all about. In actuality, I disliked
Church people in general. When I was very young, my father was a choir
director at the local Church we attended, which at that time was
pastored by a distant cousin. Being a "Church kid", I got a first row seat
of seeing the good, the bad, and the ugly in people. I grew to see that
some Church people, who were supposed to be the safest folks to be
around, turned out to be the ones always causing the most trouble. They
always seemed to be fighting and complaining. I was told to love others
by the people who seemed to have no love at all. So many times while
the choir was practicing and singing Hallelujah, I was in the back of the
Church, cussing and fighting with the other kids. Like a lot of Church
kids, I determined that ministry was in no way something that I desired.
This would soon change forever because God had other plans. He gave
me a glimpse into the spirit realm. You see, one night Jesus walked into
my bedroom and stood before me.

It was as if I walked into an invisible wall of electricity. It seemed
that I had taken a step out of this earthly realm and into the Heavenly
realm. In actuality, that night, Heaven walked into me. One moment I
was standing up getting ready to go to bed, minding my own business,
and the next moment I found myself crouched on the floor, with my
head to the ground as if something with tremendous weight was on my
back and shoulders.

I cannot say that I was in prayer or in any perceivable state of spiritual awareness. I can still vividly remember the uncontrollable tears that instantly began to pour from my eyes, rolling off of my cheeks and falling down onto the brown, sandaled feet standing in front of my head. I could slightly feel the white linen cloak which came down around two ankles, brush against my neck. At this moment, I knew I was not alone in that place.

Everything in the room seemed to have a gentle breeze of static electricity to it. Even the darkness in the room did not seem dark, though the lights were off. There I lay, with my head pushed to the floor, shaking in a bowed position as He revealed to me His overwhelming love and exchanged His thoughts with me on things concerning my future. To this day, it is hard to describe with words how this communication felt. One thing I noticed was though the room was silent, there was a perceptible low frequency buzzing that made my ears feel warm and almost deaf, drowning out even my own thoughts.

I still remember like it was yesterday, the sensation of the warmth of His glory and light wrapping over me, seeming to envelop my whole body. The unmistakable sweet yet spiced fragrance that seemed to waft into my nostrils from the inside out. Every time I breathed, it felt as though I breathed in His very presence.

I could visualize in my spirit, His eyes of inexhaustible love, gazing into my soul, as we began to exchange thoughts without words. Though He stood in silence before me, I could hear my spirit inside of me talking, almost audibly. I will never forget the feeling of the weight of His spirit resting on me like a thick, heavy blanket, pressing in upon me until I could hardly breathe. This wave of what felt like static electricity seemed to permeate and vibrate my whole body, hair and even my clothes.

Suddenly, I began to see with my eyes closed, what looked like a video screen playing before my eyes, yet I knew it was in my mind. All of the sudden, I saw several people in my church that I had known, riding in a little red car together along a small mountain road. Suddenly, the car swerved and crashed into pieces, and all of them where instantly killed (later, I would find that this accident was diverted). It was at this moment that a Holy language came out of my belly, up through my throat with such great force that it felt as if my insides where going to come out of my mouth. Instantly, I knew what was happening. *This was the prayer of intercession.* I had read about this in my Bible. The words of Romans 8:26 came flooding up to my mind *"with groanings which cannot be uttered..."*

As I continued to intercede in this new, un-known tongue, I lay on the floor for at least several hours in this sub-conscious state, praying and interceding for many other things, especially the events concerning my future. I began to pray for different people in my life, while simultaneously having knowledge of exactly where they were and who it was for.

Jesus never spoke a word to me during this first visitation, but I had an inward knowing of His thoughts. The one partial glimpse I caught of His face was very quick, as I could hardly lift up my head. Then He was gone.

The aftershock of this trembling and prayer continued for several days following this encounter. I could barely go to school the next day. I hardly spoke to anyone or did anything more than sit in silence and rehearse this experience in my heart. I did not want to lose this unexplainable closeness with The Holy Spirit or think any thought that would cause His presence to leave or lift off of me. My lips stammered almost continuously with a diverse and nearly uncontrollable language. It was during this humbling, life altering encounter that I discovered my purpose for living. This experience with Jesus was my introduction to The Holy Spirit and His gifts.

Have you ever wondered why we are seeing so few people today truly operating in the fullness of the *spiritual gifts*? I believe much of this surface Christianity is due to many lacking a true encounter with Jesus. In other words, A "Damascus Road" experience.

It is no secret that there exists, at the time of writing this book, a shortage of supernatural power being displayed in the people of the American church. If you have ever wondered about these things you are not alone. Now, more than ever, there is a deep spiritual yearning in this generation for the manifestation of God through the nine Gifts of the Spirit. The mantle (calling) has been passed, and is not meant to be kept to ourselves but rather used (2 Kings 2:14). The lighted torch seems to have fallen but I believe there is a new breed of men and women who will pick up and carry this message of the Gifts of the Spirit to the farthest reaches of the globe. One of the great apostles of the modern day Church, Dr. Lester Sumrall once said concerning the Gifts of the Spirit, *"Can you imagine Heaven giving gifts to the earth? We ought to be giving Heaven gifts for all the good things we have received."* In other words, we must do our part to populate heaven! If there has ever been a time where we, as the Church, need to rise in faith and power, it is now. The world and many in the Church are desperately searching for an encounter with the supernatural. It is disheartening to know that so many people are rapidly losing faith in God's Word and the Church and turning to witchcraft and the occult. Why is this? I believe it is because there is a shortage of people willing to step out in faith beyond the status quo and dare to believe God in fresh dimensions of faith.

Yes, the world is tired of the status quo. People are searching for real hope, real answers and real help. In striving for peace and purpose, those in the world may be unaware that what they actually need is Jesus. The most effective way to demonstrate to the world that Jesus is alive is to do what He did: *Heal their sick, raise their dead, cast out devils, speak with new tongues* (Mark 16:17-18).

The Church must rise to the occasion and step into the fullness of the faith by demonstrating the love of Jesus to the world through the mighty Gifts of the Spirit. I believe with absolute certainty, there is no greater subject to discuss, besides salvation, than the Gifts of The Holy Spirit. This message is urgently important to every born-again believer! I believe the only thing that will cause the wayward Christian and the sinner searching for their purpose in life to turn to Jesus in these final days is *the manifestation of Christ through the Gifts of the Spirit!*

Yieldedness

The Church stands at the door of the greatest move of God ever to be seen since the book of Acts, but it must begin with the Gifts of the Spirit once again flowing in and through our daily lives. Ecclesiastes 1:9

states, *"Everything that has been, will be..."* As it was at the inception of the Church, so it shall be in these final moments for the Bride of Christ. Nothing testifies of Christ's Resurrection like His mighty power in operation. In John 14:12 Jesus said, *"Greater works will you do because I go unto the Father."*

I like something I heard a man of God once state: *If we as the Church want to do what Jesus did, we must do what Jesus does.* First John 4:17 clearly states...*"as He is, so are we in the earth."* It is time to be Jesus in the earth!

Are you ready to receive the impartation of the Gifts of the Spirit? God is not looking for perfect people to use; He is looking for people who are perfectly yielded. I heard Kathryn Kuhlman, a mighty evangelist known for her "Healing and Miracle Services" once say, *"God is not looking for silver or golden vessels, He is looking for yielded vessels."* A yielded life is the key to being used in the Gifts of the Spirit. When you and I are completely yielded to the Holy Spirit's leading *spirit, soul,* and *body*, we will then be in a correct position for God to use us. Yieldedness is availability; it is simple obedience. Yieldedness says, *"Wherever you go, I will go, whatever you say, I will say."*

In today's society the problem with most people is that they are not at all present with the Lord. They are too busy receiving the next call, taking the next text message or sending that next email.

There are so many voices in the world today speaking to our minds that it makes it extremely difficult for most people to tune their spiritual ears in to the voice of God. God will never interrupt us. Instead, He will quietly wait for us to become yielded and still before He speaks.

Psalm 23 states, *"the Lord is our Shepherd."* A shepherd never pushes or prods the sheep, but always leads. For us to start being led by God's

Spirit, we must be aware of His still quiet voice—that faithful, inward witness. God never speaks to our minds; He speaks to our spirits. As recorded in 1 Corinthians 2:13, Paul wrote: *"Which things also we speak, not in the words which man's wisdom teacheth, but which the Holy Ghost teacheth; comparing spiritual things with spiritual."*

In similar wording, King David wrote in Psalms 42:7, *"Deep calleth unto deep at the noise of thy waterspouts."* Numerous times throughout the word of God water is used as a symbol for the Spirit of God. As Jesus declared in John 7: 38, *"He who believes in Me, as the Scripture has said, out of his heart will flow rivers of living water."*

The word *deep* in Psalm 42:7 speaks of water. *Deep* only cries *unto deep*; *spirit* only answers *to spirit*. The word *waterspout* used in this verse describes a tornado or cyclone over a body of water. What a great, visual representation of our relationship with God! A tornado pulls everything below itself up into the atmosphere with such great force it is actually becoming one with the water or debris that is sucked into its vortex.

This is a wonderful example of how our spirit communicates and becomes one with God. 1 Corinthians 6:17 says, *"But he that is joined unto the Lord is one spirit."* Likewise, as we yield ourselves to The Holy Spirit, God's Spirit draws us to Himself. John 6:44 states, *"No man can come to Me except the Father which has sent Me draw him."*

God does the *drawing*, we do the *yielding*. Did you ever stop to think about it: you and I, as believers, have everything we will ever need reserved inside of our spirit? God, The Holy Ghost lives in us! As we submit our life to His, there is a Heavenly exchange as we are pulled up higher and filled with all the fullness of God!

Be Transformed

Everything we do, we must do in the realm of the Spirit. Jesus said in John 4:24, *"God is a Spirit and they that worship Him must worship Him in spirit and in truth."* We are to be transformed into the image of Christ and not vice versa. Like the lyrics of the old song sings, "Have Thine own way, Lord! Have Thine own way! Thou art the potter and I am the clay! Mold me and make me after Thy will, while I am waiting, yielded and still."

Romans 8:29 says, *"for those God foreknew He also predestined to be conformed to the image of His Son."* We must allow God to transform us into His image. It is of utmost importance that we live in this state of a moldable conscience towards the things of God if we are to ever walk in the fullness of His Spirit.

God's Spirit continually pulls us to a higher realm if we will yield to the working of His mighty power. God's message to John before he ever received further revelations was *"Come up here"* (Revelation 4:1). We must first be willing to submit ourselves to God's power before we will ever be in a position to receive further blessings from the Lord. God desires an intimate relationship with you and me, but we must be available to Him. The problem is never with God; it is always us.

One truth I have learned that I believe will remedy one hundred percent of the doubt that rises up in the lives of His children is *"Good God-Bad devil."* The issue is never God not speaking or leading; the real question is: *are we listening?* The problem is not the source, but the receiver; the recipient and not the giver. The Father is continually seeking those who will commune with Him in spirit.

Charisma

I am sure there are many Christians today unaware of the importance of living a Spirit-led life. The word that best describes this vitality is the Greek word χάρισμα or charisma meaning *"grace-gift"* or *"spiritual gifts."* Xarismata (the plural form) literally means "grace-endowments." This charisma divinely empowers a believer to share God's work with others, i.e. Spirit-empowered service to the Church to carry out His plan for His people. *1 peter 4:10 As every man hath received the gift, even so minister the same one to another, as good stewards of the manifold grace of God.*

Let it be us, let it be now. Living in the Spirit is the answer that will bring an end to spiritual drought!

Galatians 5:25 says, *"If we live in the Spirit, let us also walk in the Spirit."* Let us no longer say concerning our assemblies or meetings that *"God will show up."* Rather, let's determine to show up to God's meeting in the realm of the Spirit. I believe this charisma is the key to Revival. If we would only realize that the Lord is abundantly more poised to give than we are to receive. When we understand this not only in our minds, but also in our hearts, we will see the manifestations of the Spirit be given to every man.

1 Corinthians 12:7: *But the manifestation of the Spirit is given to every man to profit withal.*

You see *every man* means *"anyone."* In Acts 10:34 Peter declared that *"God is no respecter of persons,"* but we certainly know He is a respecter of faith! He will look over a million other people to answer one who is yielded to His Spirit!

In 2 Chronicles 16:9 we read, *"For the eyes of the Lord run to and fro throughout the whole earth to show Himself strong in the behalf of them whose heart is perfect towards Him."*

Hearing and receiving from God is so simple, most Christians miss it completely! We must become as little children in our thinking and believing if we are to ever gain entrance into the kingdom of God and experience His gifts.

Become as Little Children

Mathew 18:2-4: *And Jesus called a little child unto Him and set him in the midst of them, and said verily I say unto you, except ye be converted and become as little children, ye shall not enter into the kingdom of heaven.*

We need to know that our weakness is God's strength. The apostle Paul found this truth to be the key to power when Jesus visited him in prison and declared, *"My grace is sufficient for thee: for my strength is made perfect in weakness. Most gladly, therefore, will I rather glory in my infirmities, that the power of Christ may rest upon me."* (2 Corinthians 12:9) In the same manner, let us realize that our inherent human frailty can, in actuality, provide the opportunity so that Christ may become strong in our lives. Let us become simple in our thinking so He may become mighty in us. Not only do we need to know who we are in Christ, but also to know who Christ is in us.

Time for Fresh Vision

Colossians 1:27: *To whom God would make known what is the riches of the glory of this mystery among the Gentiles, which is Christ in you the hope of glory.*

The time of ignorance concerning spiritual gifts is over. The devil has blinded the eyes of men and women long enough! It is the season for fresh vision as was prayed in Ephesians 1:18: *"The eyes of our understanding be enlightened that we might discover what is the hope of our calling in Christ Jesus."* The one thing the devil hates the most is a believer who knows who they are and what they have been given! Let us rise in faith and victory, taking our rightful place, seated together with Jesus in heavenly places.

Ephesians 2:6: *And hath raised us up together, and made us sit together in heavenly places in Christ Jesus.*

This is a beautiful place where everything He has suddenly becomes ours! Join me as we take a journey through the Word of God together. Learn what the Gifts of the Spirit are and how we can live the life God desires us to live! It is time to unlock the mystery surrounding the nine gifts of the Spirit.

CHAPTER ONE
What Are the Nine Gifts of The Holy Spirit?

To better understand the gifts of the Spirit, and more specifically, the nine gifts, it would be beneficial for us to read 1 Corinthians chapter 12. Beginning at verse one, Paul the apostle writes, *"Now concerning spiritual gifts brethren, I would not have you ignorant."*

In the King James Version of the Bible, the word *gifts* is italicized. The reason behind this specific italicization is because while the King James translators were transcribing the Greek text into the English language in 1 Corinthians 12 verse one, they realized there was no English word to substitute for the Greek word πνευματικός, ή, όν or *pneumatikos*, which means *spirituals* or *spiritual things*. The Greek word *pneumatikos* is comprised of two Greek words, *pneuma* meaning *spirit* and *tikos,* a suffix used especially in the formation of Greek adjectives. It is important to note that the King James translators were extremely careful not to alter the text of God's word; they did not want to translate incorrectly altering the meaning of the original Greek text. The translators added the English word *gifts* in italics after the word *spiritual* for the sake of clearer understanding for the reader. This addition more effectively portrays the meaning of the Greek word *pneumatikos* or *spirituals* since there is no equivalent word in the English language.

Now we are able to better comprehend the true meaning behind the words *"spiritual gifts"* in this passage and have a greater understanding of Paul's meaning when he writes to us concerning the *spiritual gifts* or *spiritual things* including, but not limited to, the nine manifestations or expressions of the Spirit of God.

Now that we have a deeper understanding of the word *gifts,* let's examine the last word in verse one of 1 Corinthians 12. Paul states, *"I would not have you ignorant."* It is saddening for me to meet so many people today, totally ignorant concerning spiritual gifts or spiritual matters. Unfortunately, just as there was ignorance in Paul's day, there is ignorance today.

Deception

Some time ago the Lord ministered to me about two levels of deception that exist among the body of believers today. The first level of deception could be defined as *ignorance* or *spiritual blindness.* The second level of deception could be defined as *a willful rejection of the truth.*

It is one thing to be innocently ignorant or unaware of the truth; but it is a totally different scenario when the truth is willfully and knowingly rejected. In my opinion, there are far too many Christians who are completely devoid of any spiritual understanding, whether through lack of exposure to the truth or through a lack of spiritual discernment.

I believe we must grab a hold of this fact: *God will never entrust His gifts to anyone who has not first learned spiritual discernment.* This is the reason I believe the gift of the *discernment of spirits* is the doorway or entrance gift to all of the remaining nine gifts of the Spirit.

Verses two and three of 1 Corinthians 12 continue, *"Ye know that ye were Gentiles, carried away unto these dumb idols, even as ye were led. Wherefore I give you to understand, that no man speaking by the Spirit of God calleth Jesus accursed and that no man can say that Jesus is Lord, but by the Holy Ghost."*

In these verses, Paul was dealing with Corinthian Christians, some who were freshly saved out of idolatry, witchcraft and sexual immorality, who in times past had operated by deceptive spirits, and were involved in soothsaying and divination. It is important to understand that the City of Corinth was a wealthy, port city known for its international sea trade and diverse, Greek culture.

Corinth was the richest port and the largest city in ancient Greece with its patron idol being poseidon, god of the sea. In light of these facts, we can clearly see why The Apostle Paul prefaced his letter on the gifts of the Spirit with a warning against idol worship. The City of Corinth was at that time, a "melting pot" of world religions and spiritual practices, many of which where brought in from oriental trading ships.

In the same manner, we must be aware and use discernment of every spiritual gift that we come into contact with so that we will not be led astray by the many anti-Christ spirits at work in our world today. Nothing from God can be "half-good" or mixed with darkness. James 1:17 says, *"Every good and perfect gift comes from above, and cometh down from The Father.."* For most everything-God has created, the devil has conjured up a counterfeit through manipulation. In the restrooms of many gas stations, a 25 cent perfume dispenser can be found. Some of the labels will read "Our version of..." These cheaper versions of a name brand cologne never smell anywhere near as good as the real thing, but actually, in my opinion, stink! Likewise, anything the devil has counterfeited never compares with God's pure manifestations. It is important to remember that not all spiritual things are from The Holy Spirit. As we learn to navigate the spirit realm, we must always be aware of what the real gifts are so as not to become spiritually "nose blind." We must walk in spiritual discernment. In 1 Corinthians 12:4 The Apostle Paul is warning us of the grave danger of falling into this trap of deception, of accepting a counterfeit version for the real thing when He writes, *"Now there are diversities of gifts, but the same Spirit"*. If a spiritual gift is from God, it will always be in unity with The Holy Spirit and His Fruit. We must test every spirit and every spiritual gift that is manifested against the Word of God. It is important to compare how an apparent spiritual gift measures up with God's Word to correctly identify its source.

I believe the best way to know whether or not a spiritual gift is from God is to listen to its message or check its "fruit."

1 Corinthians 2:15: *But he who is spiritual judges all things, yet he himself is rightly judged by no one.*

Galations 5:22-23: *But the fruit of the Spirit is love, joy, peace, longsuffering, gentleness, goodness, faith, Meekness, temperance: against such there is no law.*

God's Redemptive plan for man

James 1:17 says, *"Every good and perfect gift comes from God."* In other words, nothing that originates from God is imperfect or evil and no person operating in a spiritual gift from God will ever do so without professing Jesus. He is the author of perfection, as Hebrews 5:9 declares, *"And being made perfect, He became the author of eternal salvation unto all them that obey Him."*

It is equally important to understand that every spiritual gift centers around one thing: *God's redemptive plan for man.* For example, in the area of the prophetic, any true prophecy from God will always deal with salvation as an end result. It will have a central focus of drawing men to Jesus Christ. God never intended for the Gifts of the Spirit to be used to bring hurt to others. Too many times I have witnessed people believing they are being used in the gifts of the Spirit yet they are hurting other people. One of the primary purposes of the gifts of the Spirit is to build others up, and not tear them down. The gifts are to be used for exhortation, not extortion.

Most loving parents would not allow their child to drive an automobile before he or she has learned to properly operate a vehicle because it could potentially put everyone on the road at risk of harm, including the child. I believe God reserves the Gifts of the Spirit for those He can trust; those who are seeking to be led by the Spirit in their daily lives; those who are *sober-minded, spiritually discerning* individuals.

First Peter 5:8 says, *"Be Sober-minded, watching and praying."* A person who lives a life of power is one who lives a life of prayer, watching and discerning the source of every situation.

Manifestations of the Spirit

1 Corinthians 12:4-7: *Now there are diversities of gifts but the same Spirit. 5And there are differences of administrations, but the same Lord. 6And there are diversities of operations, but it is the same God which worketh all in all* (all these gifts in everyone) *7But the manifestation of the Spirit is given to every man to* *profit withal.*

Webster's Dictionary defines the word *manifestation* as *a perceptible, outward or visible expression.* I particularly like another definition found in Webster's: *A public demonstration of power or purpose.* This is precisely what the Gifts of the Spirit are designed to do, to provide a vehicle through which the love of Jesus can be demonstrated in the earth.

The last part of verse seven states that the manifestation of the Spirit is *given to every man to profit withal.* The nine gifts of the Spirit are not exclusive to those who stand behind a pulpit or to the *fivefold* Ministries; they are available to *everyone* who yields their life to the gentle leading of the Holy Spirit.

We must pay special attention to the words, *"There are diversities of gifts but it is the same Spirit and there are different administrations but the same Lord."*

Every spiritual gift is diverse in its nature as it reveals a different aspect of God yet the gifts become unified as they function together within The Church revealing God as one. This is a beautiful picture of how the body of Christ is unified through diversity. The Church has many members that function separately but are knit together within the same body.

Many times, people that begin to function in specific gifts seem to have a tendency of isolating themselves from the Church body. This is completely wrong. The Gifts of the Spirit will always function solely within the body of Christ, the Church. There are differences of spiritual gifts but it is the same Spirit of God. There are different administrations or governments within the Church but functioning together, they reveal the same Lord, Jesus Christ. Hence, there is no such thing as a troglodyte or "Lone-Ranger" Christian. The Gifts of The Spirit are not designed to elevate someone out of the Body of Christ rather they are purposed to work within and through the Church.

This passage continues with a list of gifts or manifestations of the Spirit.

1 Corinthians 12:8-11: *For to one is given by the spirit, the word of* **wisdom**; *to another the word of* **knowledge** *by the same spirit.* 9*To another* **faith** *by the same spirit; to another the gifts of* **healings** *by the same spirit;*10*to another the working of* **miracles**; *to another* **prophecy**; *to another* **discerning of spirits**; *to another* **divers kinds of tongues** *;to another the* **interpretation of tongues:** 11*but all these worketh that one and selfsame Spirit, dividing to* **EVERY MAN** *severally as* **He will**.

Notice the last part of verse eleven. Once again, Paul is emphasizing the fact that *everyone* (every man, woman and child) can receive an impartation of the Gifts of the Spirit as He wills! This means YOU! What Revelation so many people have seemingly missed! If we are willing to place ourselves in line with the will of God, through discernment, the Holy Spirit will divide the appropriate spiritual gift(s) needed for every situation we will ever face in our lives and Ministries, helping people to clearly see God in His fullness!

Weapons of Warfare

The gifts of the Spirit are useful weapons in spiritual warfare. 2 Corinthians 10:4 states, *"For the weapons of our warfare are not carnal, but mighty through God to the pulling down of strong holds."*

We must be keenly aware of the fact that the devil is not as concerned with attacking the gifts but rather the vessels through whom the gifts of the Spirit are flowing. The enemy is afraid of this "old dominion" (Genesis 1:28). We, as believers, represent God's dominion in the earth as we come to know our rightful position in Christ.

Ephesians 1:21: *Far above all principality, and power, and might, and dominion, and every name that is named, not only in this world, but also in that which is to come:*

Luke 10:19 *Behold, I give unto you power to tread on serpents and scorpions, and over all the power of the enemy: and nothing shall by any means hurt you.*

I am sure there is absolutely no message that will experience greater, spiritual opposition than the authority of the believer. When I was a young boy, the neighbors across the street from where I lived had four old pear trees in their front yard. I remember eating my fill of those big, sweet pears. But I will never forget the horrible swarm of flies that accompanied those pears after they hit the ground. If one day went by without harvesting those pears, the whole yard would be covered with a sticky, rotten mess. Years later, they decided to remove those beautiful old trees, partially due to their un-willingness to consistently harvest the fruit. Cutting down and uprooting those pear trees fixed the problem of the flies, but in doing so also removed the fruit. *The gifts of the Spirit produce the fruit of the church (souls).*

Moreover, *wherever there is fruit, there will also be flies!* Many churches have completely shut down the flow of the spirit in a service, for fear of someone getting in the flesh. In that church, the devil has won.

Kenneth E. Hagin, a great teacher on the subject of faith once said: *"We must learn to chew up the hay and spit out the sticks."* This same frame of mind allows us to receive from anyone God might be using, even if we might not agree with everything that they say or do. If it's the word of God, it can be received, regardless of who it is flowing through.

Let us never be found guilty of grieving The Holy Spirit in fear of someone acting out in the flesh. Always remember, God uses people. This is a good example of how the enemy works. The devil knows that in order to stop the fruit from being produced he must attack and uproot the entire tree. satan is not so much concerned with hindering someone from being healed as he is about attacking the individual through whom the gift of healing is flowing.

Have you ever stopped to think about how much time and effort is spent on attacking supply lines and shipments in a war? The devil knows that if he can eliminate the source, he can stop the supply. One of the main purposes of the Gifts of the Spirit is for the edification and perfection of the body of Christ and without them, the church would not be properly equipped.

We must reclaim our rightful place, through renewing our mind by the Word. Let us begin to live from this position of dominion, reigning as kings in the earth, seated together with Christ in heavenly places.

It is high time for the Church of Jesus Christ to rise in her authority and pull back the forces of darkness through wielding the Gifts of the Spirit.

Rightfully Receive

When Jesus ascended to the throne of the Father, He not only presented Himself as the complete sacrifice for the atonement of sin, but He also received every spiritual gift on our behalf.

Psalm 68:18: *Thou hast ascended on high, thou hast led captivity captive: thou hast received gifts for men; yea, for the rebellious also, that the LORD God might dwell among them.*

Paul writes of this same occurrence in Ephesians 4:6-8: *One God and Father of all, who is above all, and through all, and in you all.* *7But unto every one of us is given grace according to the measure of the gift of Christ.* *8Wherefore He saith, When He ascended up on high, He led captivity captive, and gave gifts unto men.* Everything that Christ received when He stood before the Father after His finished work on the Cross we now have because He received those spiritual gifts for us! The Gifts of the Spirit are for you and me if we will only take our prepared place in the Person of Jesus Christ, seated in heavenly places!

Ephesians 2:6: *And hath raised us up together, and made us sit together in heavenly places in Christ Jesus*

CHAPTER TWO
Numerical Mysteries

In our study of 1 Corinthians 12, we have discovered there are nine individual and separate gifts or expressions of the Spirit. Let us look at some examples of why the number nine is spiritually significant:

The Number Nine

In the Hebrew numeral system, the number nine or ט *Tet* is the ninth letter in the Hebrew alphabet and is the largest single-digit number in the system of numeration. In Hebrew, the letter as well as its meaning is generally accepted to be connected to the Hebrew word *Tov* (טוב), meaning *good*. While *Tet* is actually the least common letter in the Hebrew Bible, it is the initial letter in the Hebrew word *Tov*. In the Bible Tov first appears numerous times during the Genesis account of Creation. It is of great significance that God described His creation as *good* or "*Tov*" in Genesis.

Genesis 1:31: *And God saw everything that he had made and behold it was very good* (tov).

Tov is a short but infinitely extensive Hebrew word. Today's indigenous English-speakers might be vaguely familiar with tov only because of hearing the Jewish/Yiddish saying "Mazel Tov" ("Good Luck" in English). The momentous power in the word *Tov* can be clearly seen from its first use in **Genesis 1.1:1** *In the beginning God created the heaven and the earth.*

1:4 And God saw the light, that it was **good** *(tov): and God divided the light from the darkness.*

1:10 And God called the dry land Earth; and the gathering together of the waters called he Seas: and God saw that it was **good** (tov).

1:11 And God said, Let the earth bring forth grass, the herb yielding seed, and the fruit tree yielding fruit after his kind, whose seed is in itself, upon the earth: and it was so.

1:12 And the earth brought forth grass, and herb yielding seed after his kind, and the tree yielding fruit, whose seed was in itself, after his kind: and God saw that it was **good** (tov).

1:18 And to rule over the day and over the night, and to divide the light from the darkness: and God saw that it was **Good** (tov).

1:21 And God created great whales, and every living creature that moveth, which the waters brought forth abundantly, after their kind, and every winged fowl after his kind: and God saw that it was **good** (tov).

1:22 And God blessed them, saying, Be fruitful, and multiply, and fill the waters in the seas, and let fowl multiply in the earth.

1:23 And the evening and the morning were the fifth day.

1:24 And God said, Let the earth bring forth the living creature after his kind, cattle, and creeping thing, and beast of the earth after his kind: and it was so.

1:25 And God made the beast of the earth after his kind, and cattle after their kind, and every thing that creepeth upon the earth after his kind: and God saw that it was **good** (tov).

1:26 And God said, Let us make man in our image, after our likeness: and let them have dominion over the fish of the sea, and over the fowl of the air, and over the cattle, and over all the earth, and over every creeping thing that creepeth upon the earth.

1:27 So God created man in his own image, in the image of God created he him; male and female created he them.

1:28 And God blessed them, and God said unto them, Be fruitful, and multiply, and replenish the earth, and subdue it: and have dominion over the fish of the sea, and over the fowl of the air, and over every living thing that moveth upon the earth.

1:29 And God said, Behold, I have given you every herb bearing seed, which is upon the face of all the earth, and every tree, in the which is the fruit of a tree yielding seed; to you it shall be for meat.

1:30 And to every beast of the earth, and to every fowl of the air, and to every thing that creepeth upon the earth, wherein there is life, I have given every green herb for meat: and it was so.

*1:31 And God saw every thing that he had made, and, behold, it was **very good** טוֹב. מְאֹד.* (*meod-tov*) exceedingly good or abundant.

In this first chapter of the Old Testament God initiated the miraculous, perpetual motion of life. He commanded the sun to give its light, this life-giving light shined upon the earth. He separated the waters to nourish the earth. God called forth the seeds He had embedded in the soil and His creative word brought forth those seeds which contained the inherent ability to reproduce after their kind. God beheld this progression of sustainable life or *Biogenesis* and called this cycle *Tov.* I believe that we are able to clearly see the importance of the number nine through the Genesis account of creation. It is of great significance that God performed nine initial creative acts during the seven days of creation.

*1 **God Moved upon the face of the deep*** (it is important to note that the Hebrew word for moved is רָחַף (Rachaph) meaning " to grow soft, to move gently, to brood over as an eagle fluttereth over her young." **Deuteronomy 32:11**)

*2 **Light was brought forth***

*3 **Firmament (sky) was created***

*4 **The land was created***

*5 **The seed was brought forth***

*6 **Stars were lighted***

*7 **Fish and foul were created***

*8 **Beasts of the earth were created***

*9 **Man was created.***

The word Genesis **means** "Origin"; or in **Hebrew**: בְּרֵאשִׁית, "Bərēšîṯ. In biblical numerology, the number nine is the number of *finalities* or *the judgment* and it is fittingly used to define *the perfect movement of God*. As is clearly seen, the perfect movement or process of God is represented by the number nine. As pertaining to the church, the nine Gifts of the Spirit cause the Body of Christ to become complete in our function. It is of no coincidence that the average time period of a normal, human gestation is nine months or 40 weeks and is arranged into three main stages known as trimesters. In essence, the nine Spiritual Gifts are essential to the process of procreation and development within The Church organism. We as believers must yield ourselves to the working of The Holy Spirit and His gifts if we are to be complete as a body, establishing effective disciples of The Lord Jesus Christ. **Matthew**

28:19 *Therefore go and make disciples of all nations, baptizing them in the name of the Father and of the Son and of the Holy Spirit,* (NIV)

Every Christ-follower should have the single goal of procreating and developing spiritually healthy followers of Jesus. Paul the Apostle writes, *Be ye followers of me, even as I also am of Christ.* **1 Corinthians 11:1**

It is by no coincidence that the Gifts of the Spirit are nine in number, this is God's perfect process and it is exceedingly good *(Meod-Tov)!* The number nine is also the number of *those who accomplish God's divine will.* A good example of this is found in The Gospel of Mathew:

Matthew 27:46: *And about the **ninth** hour Jesus cried with a loud voice, saying, Eli, Eli, lama sabachthani? that is to say, My God, my God, why hast thou forsaken me?*

Christ died at the **ninth** hour of the day (3:00 p.m.), completing His work to make eternal redemption available to everyone who would believe on Him.

John 3:16: *For God so loved the world that He gave His only begotten Son that whosoever believes on him shall not perish but have everlasting life.*

It was also at the **ninth** hour of the day when a Roman Centurion named Cornelius was told in a spiritual vision to contact the Apostle Peter. Cornelius would eventually be baptized and receive the infilling of the Holy Spirit, becoming the first recorded Gentile to become a Christian.

Acts 10:1-8: *There was a certain man in Caesarea called Cornelius, a centurion of the band called the Italian band,* ²*A devout man, and one that feared God with all his house, which gave much alms to the people, and prayed to God alway.* ³*He saw in a vision evidently about the ninth hour of the day an angel of God coming in to him, and saying unto him, Cornelius.* ⁴*And when he looked on him, he was afraid, and said, What is it, Lord? And he said unto him, Thy prayers and thine alms are come up for a memorial before God.* ⁵*And now send men to Joppa, and call for one Simon, whose surname is Peter:* ⁶*He lodgeth with one Simon a tanner, whose house is by the sea side: he shall tell thee what thou oughtest to do.* ⁷*And when the angel which spake unto Cornelius was departed, he called two of his household servants, and a devout soldier of them that waited on him continually;* ⁸*And when he had declared all these things unto them, he sent them to Joppa.* In this same portion of Scripture, the term "*Christian*" was first used. Not coincidentally, there are also **nine** fruits of the Spirit. These spiritual fruits are found in Galatians chapter 5.

Galatians 5:22-23: *But the fruit of the Spirit is love, joy, peace, longsuffering, gentleness, goodness, faith,* ²³*meekness, temperance: against such there is no law.*

The Number Three

Since there are nine gifts of the Spirit or spiritual manifestations, we can thusly divide them into three equal parts. The number *three* in the Hebrew numeral system is ג, pronounced *shalosh* meaning *completeness* or *divine order*.

One of the many examples of the spiritual significance of the number three is found in the way we measure time: *past, present,* and *future.*

There are three general dispensations or time periods in which God has dealt with humanity. In the Old Testament, The Father dealt with man. In the New Testament Gospels, Jesus dealt with man. In the Epistles, The Holy Spirit deals with man.

Ephesians 1:10 *That in the dispensation of the fulness of times he might gather together in one all things in Christ, both which are in heaven, and which are on earth; even in him:*
The significance of the number three and the way in which it is woven into the fabric of all creation is also evident in the fact that there are 27 books in the New Testament. Twenty-seven divided by three is nine, which is 3x3x3 or *completeness to the third power.*

In the Hebrew numerical system, each letter of the alphabet has a corresponding numerical value each containing deep spiritual meanings describing God in every part of creation.

The Trinity is yet another example of the significance of the number three found in the Bible. There are three manifestation of God demonstrated through the three Persons of the Godhead: *The Father, Son,* and *Holy Spirit.*

Every fundamental attribute of creation seems to be arranged into multiples or sets of three. **The trees**: *the Bark, the Pulp, and the Sap.* **The earth**: *the core, the mantle, and the crust.*
Man is also a three-part being. God created man *in His likeness and image.* We not only bear God's completeness in our makeup but possess His image and likeness as well.

Genesis 1:27: *So God created man in His own image; in the image of God He created him; male and female He created them.*

How remarkable it is that God would choose man to become a living spirit like Him. In light of this fact, it would be difficult to ever question your worth with God! We not only look like Him but also contain the very attributes of His Soul.

As a three-part being, man is comprised of a *spirit, soul*, and *body*. This is described in 1 Thessalonians 5:23: *And the very God of peace sanctify you wholly; and I pray God your whole* **spirit, soul** *and* **body** *be preserved blameless unto the coming of our Lord Jesus Christ.*

God, in the very essence of who He is, bears the image of three, as does everything He creates. The first Hebrew word for "*God*" in the original text of Genesis chapter one is אֱלֹהִים and is transliterated as "*Elohim*," which is plural for *God* or *gods*. *Elohim* is synonymously used throughout the book of Genesis to describe God in His plural or threefold form. **Genesis 1:1** *In the beginning God created the heaven and the earth.*

The Trinity

The scriptures clearly describe God as comprised of three individual Persons: *The Father, The Son,* and *The Holy Spirit*. Through Scripture I also believe each member of the Godhead has His own soul (*mind, will, and emotions*) and distinctly separate body: The Holy Spirit possessing a spiritual body, Jesus, having a glorified body, and The Father a spirit body different than that of the Holy Spirit. A few Scriptural Examples of the description of God are:

Revelation 1:13-18 -Describes *Jesus*

Revelation 4:2-3, Revelation 5:6-7 -Provides a description of *The Father* separate from Jesus.

The Holy Spirit's name denotes that He has a spiritual body. The Bible refers to the third member of the Godhead as the *Holy Spirit*. The idea of Him being a spirit indicates that He is without physical form. In conclusion, The Word of God gives a clear description of *The Holy Trinity* being comprised of three separate individuals existing in perfect harmony.

1 John 5:7: *For there are three which bear record in heaven, the Father, the Word* (Son), *and the Holy Ghost: and these three are one.*

These *"three"* are *one*, meaning one in soul.

John 17:21: *That they all may be one; as thou, Father, art in me, and I in thee, that they also may be one in us: that the world may believe that thou hast sent me.*

Matthew 28:19: *Go ye therefore, and teach all nations, baptizing them in the name of the Father, and of the Son, and of the Holy Ghost:*

I believe each of the nine gifts of the Spirit, when separated into three categories or attributes, is the direct manifestations of the three Persons of the Godhead. In other words, the nine gifts of the Spirit are, by nature, the manifestations or expressions of God in His complete form. This is the mystery behind the nine gifts of the Spirit.

God in His Fullness Revealed

I believe when we, as the body of Christ in the earth, begin to function in all nine gifts of the Spirit, God in His fullness will be revealed in His complete form! What a powerful illumination of truth!

1 Corinthians 2:12: *Now we have received, not the spirit of the world, but the spirit which is of God; that we might know the things that are freely given to us of God.*

Remember, there is no new revelation of the Word of God, but a daily illumination of already revealed truths. These puzzle pieces of truth, when put together, reveal a clearer image God. Truth only fits together one way just like we, as the Church body, will only reveal God in His completeness when we are unified together through the operation of the nine Gifts of the Spirit. Hallelujah! This is a new light shed upon the subject of the Gifts the Spirit!

Psalm 119:105: *Thy word is a lamp unto my feet and a light unto my path.*

What will be revealed to us as we are faithful to pursue truth has already been revealed from the beginning.

Ecclesiastes 1:9: *The thing that hath been, it is that which shall be; and that which is done is that which shall be done: and there is no new thing under the sun.*

It is also important to be reminded of the fact that no revelation of truth is to be kept a secret!

2 Peter 1:20: *Knowing this first that no prophecy of scripture is of any private interpretation.*

Let us begin to walk in the light of this revealed truth and literally *manifest God* in these last days throughout the earth. Thank God for the Holy Spirit living on the inside of every believer who has yielded to His power! We can tap into His great omniscience on the inside of us; all we need to do is be tuned in and quietly listen to His instruction!

1 John 2:20: *But we have an unction from the Holy One, and we know all things.*

All means *all*, my friend, and that is exactly where God wants us to live! It is time to be as God in the world! We must walk in the light of His knowledge concerning the great Spiritual gifts He gave to mankind after the Cross.

Ephesians 4:8: *Wherefore he saith; When he ascended up on high, he led captivity captive and gave gifts unto men.*

Sons of God

Psalm 82:6: *I have said, Ye are gods; and all of you are children of the Most High.*

The greatest gift, beyond salvation, is the exclusive opportunity to portray the triune God in their completeness, through the gifts of the Spirit. In John 10:34 Jesus quoted *Psalm 82:6* and said that we are called *"gods"* in the earth. Interestingly this word *"gods"* translates into the same Hebrew word *Elohim*.

The Hebrew translation of this passage in John is בני האלהים or transliterated as bənê hā'ĕlōhîm, literally meaning *sons of Elohim*. The Greek Lexicon describes this same phrase as *sons of God*. Several times throughout the Old and New Testament we read that angels, fallen or not, are referred to as the sons of Elohim(God). However, starting in Genesis 2:4 we see God's name suddenly change from God (Elohim) to *"The Lord God"* or יְהוָה (Yahweh) אֱלֹהִים (Elohim). The use of this name demonstrates God's desire to adopt man as His own offspring. When it comes to creation, in Genesis chapter one, God did not identify Himself in connection with trees, animals or angels; only with man. Angels are not sons of Yahweh or YHVH (Yehovah) neither does the devil know God as Yah, only as Elohim.

In most cases Yahweh or Yehovah seem to be used interchangeably and is, sometimes, pronounced as Jehovah. Jehovah is a latinization of the Hebrew name Yehovah and is commonly pronounced with a "J" among English speakers. Since the early Hebrew text did not contain vowels but only consonants, the correct pronunciation of God's name is argued by some.

However, the special name of God that is given in Exodus when Moses met with God is YHWH (Yahweh), which is "I AM."

You and I are not called sons of Elohim we are called sons of Yah (short form of Yahweh). Elohim or "Sons of The Lord God".

It is also important to note that the moment God formed Adam from the dust, He became his Lord. This is the first time in The

Scripture the word Yah is used because it is mentioned in connection with man by virtue of the covenant. Man became a vessel containing the breath of life, a keeper of the Garden of God.

Genesis 2:7 *And the **Lord God** formed man of the dust of the ground, and breathed into his nostrils the breath of life; and man became a living soul.*

Elohim is God, Yahweh is my Lord. Throughout the Old Testament the prophets continually declared, "Thus sayeth The Lord." But Jesus came saying, "*verily I say,*" because He *IS* the Lord.

Moses asked God who He was in Exodus 3:13-14: *And Moses said unto God, Behold, when I come unto the children of Israel, and shall say unto them, The God of your fathers hath sent me unto you; and they shall say to me, What is his name? what shall I say unto them? And God said unto Moses, I AM THAT I AM: and he said, Thus shalt thou say unto the children of Israel, I AM hath sent me unto you.*

This phrase in the Hebrew language is אֶהְיֶה אֲשֶׁר אֶהְיֶה and is pronounced eh-yeh; asher eh-yeh (I Am who I Am). Jesus stood in the temple and declared, "I am Yah." *Jesus said unto them, "Verily, verily, I say unto you, Before Abraham was, I am."* (John 8:58) This explains why the Jews became so angry with Jesus that they wanted to crucify Him. They were offended because He called Himself God (Yah). To the unbelieving Jews this was blasphemy, but to the believers these were the words of life. Jesus is the living Word of God. Let these truths sink deep into your spiritual mind.

What an illumination! In other words, everything God possesses He has given unto us; *as He was* on the earth during His earthly ministry, *so are we* (1 John 4:17). Every gift and ability God has is available to us now through The Name of Jesus. I believe this is the will of the Lord just as Jesus prayed: *Thy kingdom come. Thy will be done on earth, as it is in heaven* (Mathew 6:9-13).

As I conclude this discussion on *numerical mysteries* found in God's Word, my hope is a greater clarity and understanding of who we are in Christ has been revealed; that we comprehend how we share the same *mathematical makeup* of God Himself and that we have learned everything God creates is in multiples of three. We can thusly conclude that the nine Gifts of the Spirit are, by numerical value, an expression of the Holy Trinity; that *the Father, the Son*, and *the Holy Spirit* each have different attributes represented through the nine Gifts of the Spirit or *spiritual manifestations.*

Made in the Image of God

Genesis 1:26-27: *And God said, let us make man in our image, after our likeness: and let them have dominion over the fish of the sea, and over the fowl of the air, and over the cattle, and over all the earth, and over every creeping thing that creepeth upon the earth. [27]So God created man in his own image, in the image of God created he him; male and female created he them.*

In examining the significance of man being made in God's image and likeness, it is vitally important that we understand the makeup of man to better see this mirror image of God.

As previously mentioned, humans are three-part beings consisting of *spirit, soul*, and *body*. I believe these three components of our makeup represent a Person in the Godhead.

First, the *spirit* of man represents the all-knowing Father in His omniscience manifesting through three of the nine gifts of the Spirit: *the word of wisdom, the word of knowledge* and *the discerning of spirits*.

Secondly, the *body* of man, I believe, represents the carnate nature of Christ, who was manifested in the flesh and came to heal the sick through gifts of healings, perform miracles through the working of miracles, and exercise the gift of faith by casting out devils, raising the dead, multiplying food, and other miraculous signs in the earth.

Finally, the *soul* of man, which is the *mind, will* and *emotions*, I believe, properly represents the vocal aspect of the Holy Spirit, relaying to the earth, the very Soul (the *mind, will*, and *emotions*) of God Himself; three separate beings in Heaven expressing their three attributes through the medium of the nine gifts of the Spirit; *nine* meaning *divine order* and *three* meaning *complete*.

In conclusion, when the individual members of the Church begin yielding to the nine gifts of the Spirit, I believe God will look down at His creation *"the Church,"* and call it *complete* in His likeness and image. This will be the moment of absolute perfection; God seeing a mirror image of Himself in the earth. Then and only then will He be able to call it *"good"* or *complete* as He did in the beginning.

I believe the resurgence of the gifts of the Spirit in the local and global church will mark the day for the great *"catching away"* of the saints.

1 Thessalonians 4:12-17: *That ye may walk honestly toward them that are without, and that ye may have lack of nothing. [13]But I would not have you to be ignorant, brethren, concerning them which are asleep, that ye sorrow not, even as others which have no hope. [14]For if we believe that Jesus died and rose again, even so, them also which sleep in Jesus will God bring with him. [15]For this we say unto you by the word of the Lord, that we which are alive and remain unto the coming of the Lord shall not prevent them which are asleep. [16]For the Lord himself shall descend from heaven with a shout, with the voice of the archangel, and with the trump of God: and the dead in Christ shall rise first: [17]Then we which are alive and remain shall be caught up together with them in the clouds, to meet the Lord in the air: and so shall we ever be with the Lord.*

CHAPTER THREE
The Expression of God

One day as I was in the study, the Lord revealed to me the significance of the Spiritual Gifts operating in the Church. As the Church of Jesus Christ, it is imperative that we begin to fully function in the Gifts of the Spirit. This is not only what we do, the gifts are our identity, but who we are. This is why Jesus said in John 14:12 that we will do *"greater works than what He did"* because our time on earth is temporary; we are to occupy until He returns!

As I have stated in the previous chapters, the more frequently the Gifts of the Spirit function in our Church pews, the more completely the body of Christ will be revealed in the earth. People must begin to be allowed to touch and see Jesus in this very real and tangible way through the Church!

1 Corinthians 13:10: *But when that which is perfect has come, then that which is in part shall be done away with.*

Hallelujah! I believe this pertains to you and me! As the Word of God clearly implies, it is possible for The Body of Christ to become so perfected by the quickening power of the Holy Spirit through the operation of the gifts, that we, as believers, are seen as a visual representation or ambassador of God in the earth.

That which currently seems to be imperfect and incomplete will suddenly exude absolute perfection, ultimately revealing Christ in the earth.

I want to examine in greater detail, each gift of the Spirit, which I believe represents God in His perfection.

Romans 8:18-19: *For I reckon that the sufferings of this present time are not worthy to be compared with the glory which shall be revealed in us.* [19]*For the earnest expectation of the creature waiteth for the manifestation of the sons of God.*

To illustrate and for the sake of clearer understanding, the nine Gifts of the Spirit will be separated into three distinct categories, each representing the three Persons of the Godhead: *God the Father, God the Son,* and *God the Holy Spirit.*

Note:

For the sole purpose of this book, I have arranged the nine Gifts of the Spirit into three sets of three. They are not categorized by biblical order, but only for the purpose of better understanding their individual qualities and uses and how they correlate with one another. I believe these three categories each represent the individual attributes of the individual members of the Godhead: God the Father, God the Son, and God the Holy Spirit.

VISUAL GIFTS
THE FATHER

Word of Wisdom
Word of Knowledge
Discerning of Spirits

VOCAL GIFTS
HOLY SPIRIT

Tongues
Interpretation of Tongues
Prophecy

THE CHURCH
BODY

VIRTUE GIFTS
THE SON

Gifts of Healings
Working of Miracles
Gift of Faith

CHAPTER FOUR
The Visual Gifts

The category of the *Visual Gifts* of the Spirit is sometimes referred to as the *Revelation Gifts*. These gifts represent the Father in His eternal wisdom and knowledge. Everything the Father created He sees. He is the Omnipotent One who dwells in an unapproachable light as described in 1 Timothy 6:16: *Who only hath immortality, dwelling in the light which no man can approach unto; whom no man hath seen, nor can see: to whom be honour and power everlasting. Amen.*

The omnipotent Father is the originator of everything good; He has always been and always will be. The Webster's Dictionary defines the word *omnipotent* as *having a virtually unlimited authority or influence.* The eyes of the Father see everything that has ever been or ever will be created. Simply put, His existence is truly beyond human comprehension.

As the age-old human question asks: *Who made God and where did He come from?* The fact is, God has always been and always will be. We have no need to understand God's existence. David said in Psalm 131:1, *"LORD, my heart is not haughty, nor mine eyes lofty: neither do I exercise myself in great matters, or in things too high for me."*

God the Father is the *Ancient of Days* who simply *IS.*

Daniel 7:9-10: *I beheld till the thrones were cast down, and the Ancient of days did sit, whose garment was white as snow, and the hair of his head like the pure wool: his throne was like the fiery flame, and his wheels as burning fire. 10A fiery stream issued and came forth from before him: thousands upon thousands ministered unto him, and ten thousand times ten thousand stood before him: the judgment was set, and the books were opened.*

Limitless Power

The heavenly Father is the One with whom there has never been nor ever will be a limitation of any kind. It seems He has never left His throne nor ever traded His attributes of limitless power. He is the One who sent forth His creative Word in the beginning. The Father is the omniscient, omnipresent entity of the universe who has never changed in form nor function.

John chapter 1 states: *In the beginning was the Word and Word was with God and the Word was God.* Notice the word *with*. We know Jesus is the Living Word that became flesh.

John 1:14: *And the Word was made flesh, and dwelt among us, (and we beheld his glory, the glory as of the only begotten of the Father,) full of grace and truth.*

The Heavenly Father is the One from whom creative word flows. When He speaks, things *become*.

Genesis 1:1: *In the beginning God created the heaven and the earth.*

The Father is the all-powerful speaking Deity. From His mouth proceeds the Living Word.

As Jesus said in John 12:49:*"For I have not spoken of myself; but the Father which sent me, he gave me a commandment, what I should say, and what I should speak."* The Word, which is Jesus, proceeded from the mouth of the Father.

John 8:42: *Jesus said unto them, If God were your Father, you would love me, for I proceeded forth and came from God; neither came I of myself but he sent me.*

All wisdom and knowledge flow forth and originate from the Father. He is the originator of all things.

Colossians 1:17: *He is before all things and by him, all things consist. .*

Sent Directly from the Father

John 7 reveals that man can only experience so much of God's revelation at a time.

John 7:15-16: *And the Jews marveled, saying, How knoweth this man letters, having never learned? Jesus answered them, and said, My doctrine is not mine, but his that sent me.*

As John declared, *No man has seen the God* (the Father) *at any time.*

John 1:18: *No one has seen God at any time; the only begotten Son, which is in the bosom of the Father, He hath declared Him.*

John 6:46: *Not that any man hath seen the Father, save he which is of God, He hath seen the Father.*

These verses establish the fact that Jesus was sent directly from the Father. God the Father is so holy and multi-faceted in His character, I believe we have not comprehended the depths of who He actually is. Jesus said to Philip, *"Jesus saith unto him, Have I been so long time with you, and yet hast thou not known me, Philip? he that hath seen me hath seen the Father; and how sayest thou then, Show us the Father?,"* but still, like Philip, we struggle in our understanding. However, there is coming a day, when we will see Him in His glory!

Revelation 20:4: *And I saw thrones, and they sat upon them.*

Someday soon, we will see and experience Him in all of His fullness, Hallelujah! Seeing now that the Father God is omnipresent (present in all places at all times) and omniscient, it is clear that He knows how to deal with any situation. As Proverbs 5:21 states, *"For the ways of man are before the eyes of the Lord and he ponderous all his doings."*

2 Chronicles16:9: *For the eyes of the Lord run to and fro throughout the whole earth, to shew himself strong in the behalf of them whose heart is perfect toward him.*

The attributes of the Father are clearly seen and understood through the category of the *Visual Gifts* of the Spirit. Again, this is why it is of utmost importance for the Church to begin to function in the nine Gifts of the Spirit.

The world must see a completed, perfected image of God Himself. When the *Visual Gifts* of the Spirit begin to function, the natural man begins to see into the realm of God. He is able to know things far beyond the scope of his current level of knowledge or understanding. The limitations in vision dealing with the past, present, and future are removed. It is through the *Visual Gifts* that the attributes of the all-seeing Father are experienced. Hebrews 4:13 states: *Neither is there any creature that is not manifest in his sight: but all things are naked and opened unto the eyes of him with whom we have to do.*

By the power of the Holy Spirit, the gift of the *word of knowledge* makes possible the ability to see situations through all-seeing eyes of the Father.

The gift of the *word of wisdom* taps into the Father's limitless ability of knowing how to deal with any circumstance.

The gift of the *discerning of spirits* is God's ability to know and reveal to man, by the Holy Spirit, every spirit at work within any particular situation; He created all beings in the beginning and though some willfully departed from God's original intention, all spirits are His creation.

We will now examine, in further detail, each of the Visual Gifts.

Word of Wisdom

Strong's Concordance defines the word wisdom as skill in the management of affairs. The Greek word for wisdom is σοφία, ας, ἡ transliterated as Sophia. The word Sophia is the root for the English terms sophistication and philosophy. We must first understand that there exists two forms of wisdom and for the sake of better understanding, I will separate them into two categories: general wisdom and the word of wisdom. General wisdom can be defined as understanding how to deal correctly with the affairs of life. The best way to receive this type of general or "life" wisdom is to ask God.

James 1:4-5: *"But let patience have her perfect work, that ye may be perfect and entire, wanting nothing. If any man lacketh wisdom, let him ask of God, that giveth to all men liberally, and upbraideth not; and it shall be given him."* In reading the fourth verse in James chapter one, you will notice that he is talking about lacking nothing in things pertaining to the affairs of this life. As we read the rest of this chapter in James, we see that He goes on to say in James 1:7, *"let not that man think he will receive anything from the Lord."* Again, James is emphasizing that we need to ask God for wisdom so that we may receive those everyday things that we have need of. In dealing with general wisdom, it is important to remember that God is the originator of all wisdom both natural and spiritual. But wisdom in dealing with the natural world is not the Spiritual gift of the word of wisdom. Many try to say that Solomon had the "gift of the word of wisdom" but this is untrue.

1 Kings 3:9 *"Give therefore thy servant an understanding heart to judge thy people, that I may discern between good and bad: for who is able to judge this thy so great a people?"*

Solomon's wisdom came because he asked of God for it. This is the general-life wisdom given to *"all men liberally"* according to how they ask. This type of wisdom deals specifically with the ability to know right from wrong within the affairs of everyday life. Now let's look at the difference between "general wisdom" from God and the Word of Wisdom.

Firstly, no one "owns" the gift of the word of wisdom or the gift of the word of knowledge otherwise they would be all-knowing, all of the time. Notice when speaking of the word of wisdom and knowledge within the context of the nine Gifts of the Spirit, Paul the Apostle uses "the word of wisdom" and "the word of knowledge" to denote the fact that they are singular. 1 Corinthians 12:8 states, *"For to one is given by the Spirit the word of wisdom; to another the word of knowledge by the same Spirit."* In other words, As the Holy Spirit divides the gift of the word of wisdom or knowledge to an individual, he or she receives just that part of wisdom or knowledge that God wants them to know, hence the words "to one is given." When we get to verse eleven of First Corinthians chapter twelve, we see Paul the Apostle conclude on how these Gifts of the Spirit are given and to whom they are given to, *"But all these worth that one and the selfsame Spirit, dividing to every man severally as he will."* Notice the words *"as he will."* This explains that the word of wisdom does not come from asking but is given to an individual as the Holy Spirit wills. The word of wisdom and knowledge are specific supernatural manifestations.

Furthermore, the nine Gifts of the Spirit are not derived from natural sources or by natural means. Natural knowledge can be gained by reading a book, just as natural wisdom can be gained by asking God. The wisdom and knowledge that comes through the Gifts of the Spirit are revealed, pertinent pieces of information, given directly from God's mind concerning His divine will. For instance, when I was younger, I would help my father work on cars. I was the gofer meaning: my job was to "Go-for" tools and his job was to do the actual fixing. It would not have been helpful if I had brought all the tools in the box when he only needed a specific one. When God divides to you a word of His wisdom, it will be only the word that is needed for the task at hand.

In conclusion, the word of wisdom is a supernatural revelation of God's divine purpose. The Spiritual Gifts are just that, they are spiritual, hence they are spiritually received!

It is important to note that in many instances, two or three Gifts of the Spirit will function together. For example, in the realm of a word of prophecy, many times the gift of the word of wisdom and the word of knowledge will also be working simultaneously. A great example of this is found in **Acts 9:10-18:**

10 And there was a certain disciple at Damascus, named Ananias; and to him said the Lord in a vision, Ananias. And he said, Behold, I am here, Lord.

11 And the Lord said unto him, Arise, and go into the street which is called Straight, and enquire in the house of Judas for one called Saul, of Tarsus: for, behold, he prayeth,

12 And hath seen in a vision a man named Ananias coming in, and putting his hand on him, that he might receive his sight.

13 Then Ananias answered, Lord, I have heard by many of this man, how much evil he hath done to thy saints at Jerusalem:

14 And here he hath authority from the chief priests to bind all that call on thy name.

15 But the Lord said unto him, Go thy way: for he is a chosen vessel unto me, to bear my name before the Gentiles, and kings, and the children of Israel:

16 For I will shew him how great things he must suffer for my name's sake.

17 And Ananias went his way, and entered into the house; and putting his hands on him said, Brother Saul, the Lord, even Jesus, that appeared unto thee in the way as thou camest, hath sent me, that thou mightest receive thy sight, and be filled with the Holy Ghost.

18 And immediately there fell from his eyes as it had been scales: and he received sight forthwith, and arose, and was baptized.

We see how Ananias was a certain disciple, not an apostle, prophet, evangelist, pastor or teacher. He was just a "certain disciple!" Praise God that anyone can be used in the Gifts of the Spirit! As we read on, you will notice that Ananias not only knew the name of the street but also the exact house where Paul was staying. This was the word of knowledge in operation. Furthermore, we see that Ananias knew the purpose behind his visit. This was the word of wisdom. Finally, we see that Ananias spoke the things that the Lord had told him to speak. This is was the word of prophecy. It is also important to note that any of the visual gifts can come through dreams, visions or an inward/audible voice.

A good example of "general" wisdom or knowledge working together in a natural way can be seen when you look at how God has given modern man the ability to access incredible knowledge. For example, technological advancements are rapidly increasing; but without God's supernatural wisdom, especially in the realm of weapons of warfare, man could devastate the earth as we know it today. Knowledge enables man to build weapons, but wisdom empowers man to properly utilize them, keeping man from blowing himself off of the planet!

The differences between natural wisdom and the word of wisdom are very evident. We as the Church must not be satisfied with natural wisdom only. We should ask the Lord for his help in positioning ourselves for The Holy Spirit to divide to us the gift of the word of wisdom. General wisdom deals with the intellect but the word of wisdom reveals God's purpose for man in spiritually specific ways. It is vitally important now, more than ever, for the Church body to begin to function is this wisdom gift. The omniscience of God The Father is made manifest when the word of wisdom is in operating in our lives. The Holy Spirit reveals the purpose of God for the church through the word of wisdom!

Next, I want to examine the word of knowledge and how this gift of the Spirit reveals God the Father in His omniscience.

Word of Knowledge

Before we understand what the word of knowledge is, we must first examine the specific meaning behind the word "knowledge." The Greek word for knowledge is gnosis. Strong's Concordance defines gnosis as to experientially know. This knowledge is gleaned from a firsthand, personal experience. It is the product of connecting theory to application. The word knowledge is also defined by Webster's Dictionary as the fact or condition of knowing something with familiarity gained by experience or association; the fact or condition of being aware of something (conscious).

Like we learned concerning wisdom, there are two different types of knowledge. Firstly, there is an intellectual knowledge that comes from observation and learning. Natural knowledge is gained through the intellect by exercising the five senses: sight, sound, smell, taste and touch. Intellectual knowledge is available to everyone on the earth according to how they live, what they see or read, and how conscious they become of the natural world around them.

Secondly, there is, what I will call, a general, spiritual knowledge that comes directly from God. This spiritual knowledge is available to every Christian and comes from the mind of God and into our spirit, through reading His Word. Psalm 119:105 *"Thy word is a lamp unto my feet, and a light unto my path."*

Have you ever been driving along in your car when all of the sudden you have an inward knowing or feeling to make a sudden correction in your route, possibly avoiding a future collision? You had no natural knowledge of any apparent danger, yet because of that inward awareness you altered your route. This is a great example of the difference between intellect and spirit knowledge.

Thirdly, there is the word of knowledge. The word of knowledge is just that, it's a "word" or piece of specific information given directly from God, exclusive of any outside influence and is for a particular situation. As born again believers, the all knowing Spirit of God lives on the inside of you but this ever-present knowledge is not the gift of word of the word of knowledge as mentioned in: 1 Corinthians 12:8 *"to another the word of knowledge by the same Spirit;"*

Furthermore, this general, spiritual knowledge is sometimes referred to as a conscience and should help us govern our daily lives. The more your mind is "cleansed" by reading God's Word, the more your spirit or inward man will be able to lead you safely along the road of life.

Romans 12:2 *And be not conformed to this world: but be ye transformed by the renewing of your mind, that ye may prove what is that good, and acceptable, and perfect, will of God.*

It is equally important to remember that not only will your born-again, human spirit tell you right from wrong, but God's Spirit living inside of your spirit will guide you as well. Let us become more in-tune to the "sound" of His voice.

Proverbs 20:27 *The spirit of man is the candle of the Lord, searching all the inward parts of the belly.*

The more you know, the better you do! When we renew our minds through reading the Word of God, we will experience the life that God desires for us in every area of our being—*spirit, soul and body* (1 Thessalonians 5:23). This is why many people are lacking purpose and direction in their lives. God said in **Hosea 4:6,** "*My people are destroyed for lack of knowledge:*" We must live our lives according to the knowledge of God's Word if we desire to experience abundant living! This is what I have defined as a general, spiritual knowledge that is available to every believer.

1 John 2:20: *But ye have an unction from the Holy One, and ye know all things.*

Proverbs 2: *For the Lord gives wisdom and out of his mouth cometh knowledge and understanding.*

Now that we have learned the three types of knowledge, let's take a look at the second of the nine Spiritual Gifts, the word of knowledge!

The word of knowledge can be defined as a divine revelation of specific realities or facts within the mind of God. It is important to understand that the word of knowledge is a supernatural manifestation of a direct thought from God's mind concerning people, places or things. It has nothing to do with things you or I might already know in the natural realm. A good example of this spiritual gift in operation can be seen working in the life of Jesus in the fourth chapter of John:

John 4:7-29 *7 There cometh a woman of Samaria to draw water: Jesus saith unto her, Give me to drink.*

8 (For his disciples were gone away unto the city to buy meat.)

9 Then saith the woman of Samaria unto him, How is it that thou, being a Jew, askest drink of me, which am a woman of Samaria? for the Jews ave no dealings with the Samaritans.

10 Jesus answered and said unto her, If thou knewest the gift of God, and who it is that saith to thee, Give me to drink; thou wouldest have asked of him, and he would have given thee living water.

11 The woman saith unto him, Sir, thou hast nothing to draw with, and the well is deep: from whence then hast thou that living water?

12 Art thou greater than our father Jacob, which gave us the well, and drank thereof himself, and his children, and his cattle?

13 Jesus answered and said unto her, Whosoever drinketh of this water shall thirst again:

14 But whosoever drinketh of the water that I shall give him shall never thirst; but the water that I shall give him shall be in him a well of water springing up into everlasting life.

15 *The woman saith unto him, Sir, give me this water, that I thirst not, neither come hither to draw.*

16 *Jesus saith unto her, Go, call thy husband, and come hither.*

17 *The woman answered and said, I have no husband. Jesus said unto her, Thou hast well said, I have no husband:*

18 *For thou hast had five husbands; and he whom thou now hast is not thy husband: in that saidst thou truly.*

19 *The woman saith unto him, Sir, I perceive that thou art a prophet.*

20 *Our fathers worshipped in this mountain; and ye say, that in Jerusalem is the place where men ought to worship.*

21 *Jesus saith unto her, Woman, believe me, the hour cometh, when ye shall neither in this mountain, nor yet at Jerusalem, worship the Father.*

22 *Ye worship ye know not what: we know what we worship: for salvation is of the Jews.*

23 *But the hour cometh, and now is, when the true worshippers shall worship the Father in spirit and in truth: for the Father seeketh such to worship him.*

24 *God is a Spirit: and they that worship him must worship him in spirit and in truth.*

25 *The woman saith unto him, I know that Messias cometh, which is called Christ: when he is come, he will tell us all things.*

26 *Jesus saith unto her, I that speak unto thee am he.*

27 *And upon this came his disciples, and marvelled that he talked with the woman: yet no man said, What seekest thou? or, Why talkest thou with her?*

28 *The woman then left her waterpot, and went her way into the city, and saith to the men,*

29 *Come, see a man, which told me all things that ever I did: is not this the Christ?*

***30** Then they went out of the city, and came unto him.*

Jesus couldn't have known in the natural that this woman had lied concerning being married. Not only did Jesus reveal that she was lying, He told her how many men she had lived with previously. Jesus had never met this woman before. Jews and Samaritans hardly had interactions in that day. This was the word of knowledge functioning in Christ's earthly ministry. If you read on in verse thirty, you will see that this woman went and told all of her family and friends what had happened and consequentially everyone came out of their houses to hear what Jesus had to say. The Gifts of the Spirit are tools in reaching the lost! It is important to note: The word of knowledge deals specifically with the past and present. The word of wisdom deals with things concerning the present and future. The word of wisdom is God revealing His divine purpose and will for mankind! It was through the word of knowledge that Jesus revealed the woman's sin, but through the word of wisdom, He revealed His present and future plan of redemption.

John 4:23: *But the hour cometh, and now is, when the true worshippers shall worship the Father in spirit and in truth: for the Father seeketh such to worship him.*

Now let's look at how the word of knowledge reveals the omniscient nature of God the Father!

The Heavenly Father is omniscient; He knows everything. There is no limit to His knowledge because He is the creator of all things. He has always and will always know the beginning to the end. He has never lacked in His omniscience.

Matthew 24:35-36: *Heaven and earth will pass away, but my words shall not pass away. But of that day and hour no man knoweth, no, not the angels of heaven, but my father only.*

It is important to understand that the omniscient attributes of the Father are clearly seen through the operation of the word of knowledge. Strong's Concordance defines the Word *omniscience* as *the state of having total knowledge, the quality of knowing everything.* For God to be sovereign over all His creation, visible and invisible, He must have the quality of omniscience. At this time, the Father, Son, and Holy Spirit are all, by nature, omniscient.

1 John 3:20: *For if our heart condemn us, God is greater than our heart, and knows all things.*

In Acts 1:7 Jesus said, *"It is not for you to know the times or the seasons, which the Father hath put in his own hands."* While He was on the earth as man, even Jesus did not have knowledge of certain times or seasons of His own coming. He temporarily traded His kingly garments and omniscience to become a man limited by His humanity but with the same access to God we have today.

Philippians 2:6-7: *Who, being in the form of God, thought it not robbery to be equal with God: but made himself of no reputation, and took upon him the form of a servant, and was made in the likeness of men.*

In **Romans 11:33** Paul says, *"O the depth of the riches both of the wisdom and knowledge of God! How unsearchable able are His judgments, and his ways past finding out!"* The depth of knowledge possessed by God the Father is so deep, that I suppose we will spend eternity learning about who the Father really is.

His attributes are so inexhaustible, even the cherubim and seraphim can only cry "*Holy!*" as they fly perpetually around God's throne.

Revelation 4:8: *Each of the four creatures had six wings and was covered with eyes all around, even under its wings, Day and night they never stop saying, Holy, holy, Holy is the Lord God Almighty who was, who is, and is to come.*

God the Father is the epitome of knowledge. Through our connection with the Holy Spirit, we too, can occasionally tap into this inexhaustible knowledge! Colossians chapter 2 sums up this subject of knowledge perfectly!

Colossians 2:2-3: *That their hearts might be comforted, being knit together in love and unto all riches of the assurance of understanding to the acknowledgment of the mystery of God and of the Father and of Christ in whom are hid all the treasures of wisdom and knowledge.*

Finally, I want to examine the last of what I have labeled the *Visual Gifts* by more closely examining the gift of the discerning of spirits!

The Discerning of Spirits

Before we dive into this particular Visual Gift of the Spirit, we must have a deeper understanding of what it is and how it functions in the life of the believer. The *discerning of spirits* is the supernatural ability to identify or discern or literally "see" spirits at work in the realm of the Spirit.

There are three types of spirits in existence: 1) *God's Spirit* 2) *evil spirits* 3) *human spirits.*

Over the years, I have encountered many people in excess concerning this gift. In my opinion, it is important to stay in the middle of the road concerning the discerning of spirits so we, as believers, will not fall off to one side or the other and get stuck in a spiritual ditch.

In my years of pastoring I have witnessed, numerous times, individuals claiming to function in the gift of *discernment of spirits*, but upon my closer examination, I discovered they themselves were the *spirit* they were *discerning*. I heard it once said that if most Christians claiming to function frequently in the *discerning of spirits* would, for one week, turn the looking glass on themselves, most of them would never desire to "*discern*" again!

Matthew 7:3-5 declares, *And why beholdest thou the mote that is in thy brother's eye, but considerest not the beam that is in thy own eye? Or how wilt thou say to thy brother, let me pull out the mote of thine eye; and, behold, a beam is in thine own eye? Thou hypocrite, first cast out the beam that is in thine own eye, and then thou shalt see clearly to cast out the mote of thy brother's eye.*

God sees and knows all spirits, both the good and the bad, simply because He created all of them. God is able, through His omniscience, to deal with each one according to His great knowledge. This is why I believe the gift of *discerning of spirits* is the doorway gift to all the other spiritual gifts.

The *gift of discernment* allows the believer the capacity to clearly identify and correctly deal with any problem at hand. The gift of the *discerning of spirits* allows the believer the ability to spiritually discern the origin of spirits, whether they be from God or from another spiritual source. I believe this fact is brought to light in John's epistle.

1 John 4:1: *Beloved, believe not every spirit, but try the spirits whether they are of God: because many false prophets have gone out into the world,* *²Hereby ye know the Spirit of God: everyone that confesseth that Jesus Christ has come in the flesh is from God.*

This gift of *discerning of spirits* is vital in the life and ministry of every Spirit-filled believer. I believe we must first be endued with this wonderful gift before we are able to correctly identify the spiritual need at its source; so we may efficiently and effectively direct our spiritual *"edge,"* the sword of the Spirit!

Some years ago I was invited to speak at a church in Arkansas that was pastored by a friend of mine. It was a Wednesday night and the meeting was completely full. I was in the middle of a healing message when suddenly, I heard a young boy's voice began to cackle and laugh coming from the middle front row. The boy stood up and began to come towards me, completely disrupting the meeting, as all attention was now on him and my response. He was laughing hysterically all the while blurting out loudly *"You can't cast me out! No one can help me, I'm full of demons!"*

At first, I paid no attention to him, but as he soon realized I was un-phased by his outburst, he became louder and louder until I could no longer speak over his display. As you can imagine, at this point the entire congregation forgot completely about the service and began staring at me to see how I would handle the situation.

I stepped forward and proceeded to cast the devil out of this poor, tormented boy, which was the only thing that came to my mind to do. But as soon as I began to lift my voice, I heard the inward voice of God speak saying, *"The boy does not have a devil; he is from a broken home and completely deprived of love and attention. He is crying out for affection anywhere and anyway he can."*

To the utter shock and bewilderment of the crowd, I began to instruct a nearby usher to seat the boy and not allow him to interrupt the service again. You should have seen the look on all of the faces of the people! I can imagine them thinking to themselves: *Is this man of God not going to set this obviously demon possessed boy free?*

Needless to say, I got very few handshakes after the service that night. After the service, just as I was on my way out the door, the associate pastor approached me and whispered in my ear something I'll never forget; he said to me *"In all the years I have been in this church and through all the speakers we have had come through, you are the only one to recognize and deal with this young man's real need. You are a man of God."*

I later learned everyone knew the issue with the boy, but were waiting to see how I would respond. I also discovered that every guest speaker who had ever tried to minister in that church was plagued by the same boy and every service conducted in that church had been disrupted and abruptly halted due to trying to *"cast out a demon"* that was not present in the first place.

Praise the Lord for the operation of the gift of the *discerning of spirits*. If we will only learn to rely fully upon the Lord, He will never let us down. I heard it said once, *"If you and I will stick with the Holy Ghost, we will never look stupid!"*

I believe it is so very important for us to yield ourselves to the *discerning of spirits* if God is to use us further in any of the other spiritual gifts. It is like a doctor, just because he can legally write prescriptions, it does not negate the fact that he still needs to know how to use them properly to utilize the authority he has been given.

Each case is different and as we learn to yield to God's power, His Spirit will lead us further into *all truth* on how to discern and properly deal with every situation that we will ever face. He is an *ever-present help in time of need!*

John 16:13: *Howbeit when He, the Spirit of truth, has come, he will guide you into all truth: for he shall not speak of himself; but whatsoever he shall hear, that shall he speak: and he will shew you things to come.*

I believe the *Visual Gift* category of spiritual gifts displays the omnipresent and omniscient nature of God the Father by allowing us to see glimpses of what He sees as His Spirit wills.

As we dive deeper into our study of the Gifts of the Spirit, I want to examine the second category of the Gifts of the Spirit that I have labeled the *Virtue Gifts*.

CHAPTER FIVE
The Virtue Gifts

The *Virtue Gifts* of the Spirit are often referred to as the *"power gifts."* These gifts play a vital role in the end-time Church.

The Greek word for *power* is δύναμις, εως, ἡ and is transliterated as *dunamis* meaning *power, might, strength* or *virtue*. The relative word *dynumi* means *to show power* and is where we derive the word for the explosive *dynamite*. The Webster's Dictionary defines the word *power* as *the ability to act or produce an effect*. Every believer should be able to give evidence to what we believe, in essence *producing results*. As the old saying goes, *"The proof is in the pudding!"*

Virtue Gifts Demonstrated

The gospel of Luke recounts the story of a woman who dealt with a physical condition in her body for twelve years with no relief.

Luke 8:43-48: *And a woman having an issue of blood twelve years, which had spent all her living upon physicians, neither could be healed of any, 44came behind him, and touched the border of his garment: and immediately her issue of blood stanched* (stopped). *45And Jesus said, Who touched me? When all denied, Peter and they that were with him said, Master, the multitude throng thee and press thee, and sayest thou, Who touched me? 46And Jesus said, Somebody, hath touched me: for I perceive that virtue is gone out of me. 47And when the woman saw that she was not hid, she came trembling and falling down before him, she declared unto him before all the people for what cause she had touched him, and how she was healed immediately. 48And he said unto her, Daughter, be of good comfort: thy faith hath made thee whole; go in peace.*

What a remarkable proclamation Jesus made when He said, *"Somebody hath touched me for I perceive that virtue is gone out of me."* The original word used in Greek for this English word *virtue* in verse 46 is *power* or d*ynamis*.

The purpose of the Virtue Gifts is to physically demonstrate God's power in the earth. We must always remember that the gifts of the Spirit are just that, they are *spiritual*. We understand from the Word of God that the physical world came from the supernatural invisible world. **Hebrews 11:3** states, *"Through faith we understand that the worlds were framed by the word of God, so that the things which are seen where not made of things which do appear.*

The Living Word

We must understand that the Word of God is the greatest power in the universe and by this Word all things are upheld in existence.

Hebrews 1:2-3 states that *"all things are upheld by the Word of His power"*. Colossians 1:16-17 similarly says, *"He* (Jesus) *is before all things and by him, all things hold together."* Hallelujah! Jesus is the powerful Word of God!

We see this in John 1:1: *In the beginning, was the Word, and the Word, was with God and the Word was God. ²the same was at the beginning with God. ³All things were made by him, and without him was not anything made that was made.*

Jesus Christ is the Living Word of God! Just as God the Father is the sovereign, speaking Person on the throne who thinks and speaks things into existence, Jesus Christ is the living Word of power that proceeds from the Father to cause things to come into being. The Father speaks the Word, the Word goes forth, and things are created. Without a doubt, John chapter 1 gives us a New Testament perspective of Genesis 1, from the book of Moses, through the eyes of Spirit-filled John! These two books perfectly describe this harmony between the Father and the Word (Jesus). Mathew 13:17 tells us *"...many prophets and righteous men have desired to see those things which ye see, and have not seen them; and to hear those things which ye hear, and have not heard them."*

John 1:4 states, *"In him was life; and the life was the light of men."* What a divine parallel between the natural creation of the world in Genesis, and the supernatural regeneration of mankind. Both the earth and man sat in darkness, cold and hopeless; Genesis 1 says *"without form and void"*. But then, through the darkness of despair, the light of the glorious Word shined unto us and brought new light and life.

Colossians 1:13 declares of God, *"Who hath delivered us from the power of darkness and hath translated us into the kingdom of his dear Son."*

God has *called us out of darkness and brought us into His marvelous light* giving us a bright destiny and purpose! I believe the description of the first moments of creation in Genesis 1 parallels perfectly with the first moments of "re-creation" in the life of redeemed man!

The Apostle John, through the Holy Spirit's revelation, gives us a picture of the creative power of the sent Word (Jesus), which in the beginning brought about creation, and at salvation brings regeneration! Hallelujah! There is power in the Living Word!

Now that we have established that Jesus is the sent Word, I want to examine and present a good analogy for how the Trinity functions together. Just as we are *spirit, soul* and *body* beings, which function together in perfect harmony, each having a separate task, so do *the Father, the Son*, and *the Holy Spirit*.

For the sake of understanding, imagine that the Father represents our mind. Everything we say or do starts as a thought. Everything that you or I fail to speak will fail to happen. As the saying proclaims, *"A thought unspoken, dies unborn."* In other words, everything we will ever do comes from something we have previously spoken and everything we speak is the direct representation of something we have chosen to think.

This is why Proverbs declares: *"For as he thinketh in his heart, so is he:"* (Proverbs 23:7)

Contrary to some opinions, we cannot separate words from thoughts. The Father is inseparable from His Word, which is Jesus. In the same way, the Holy Spirit is inseparable from the Word, who is Jesus. The Father spoke the Word, Jesus went forth, and the Holy Spirit caused things to be created and formed.

Genesis 1:2 states, *"And the Spirit of God* רוּחַ *"Ruach"* (the Holy Spirit) *moved upon the face of the waters."*

Jesus also gave an example of this in John 16:13 *"Howbeit when he, the Spirit of truth has come, he will guide you into all truth: for he shall not speak of himself;* (the Holy Spirit) *but whatsoever he shall hear, that shall he speak: and he will show you things to come."*

Jesus is the Word who accomplishes the will and purpose of the Father. Acts 10:38 says of Jesus, *"How God anointed Jesus of Nazareth with the Holy Ghost and with power: who went about doing good, and healing all that were oppressed of the devil; for God was with him."*

Jesus functioned in the nine Gifts of the Spirit. Included in those gifts are the *Virtue Gifts* of the Spirit! I want to examine the characteristics of those *Virtue Gifts.*

The *Virtue Gifts include: Gifts of Healings, Working of Miracles and The Gift of Faith* = Jesus, the Living Word.

The Gifts of Healings

The definition of the word *healing* in Webster's Dictionary is *the act or process of curing or restoring to health.* The Greek word for *healing* is ἴαμα pronounced as *iama* in English and comes from the word *iaomai* meaning *a cure* (the effect).

By this definition, the difference between the gifts of healings and the working of miracles is clarified. For the sake of simplification, healing is the restoration of something that was broken or damaged, or a condition that is cured. The gifts of healings is the supernatural restoration of the human body through divine intervention.

The gifts of healings should be readily more understood than some of the other gifts of the spirit due to its self-explanatory nature. As the name implies, the gifts of healings have to do specifically with the supernatural removal of disease and the restoration of the body, outside of natural means.

It is important to note that the gifts of healings are in no way connected to medical science, medicinal cures, naturopathic medicine or foods. Yes, I believe that God has provided us many natural ways of "curing" physical ailments but we must separate Divine Healing from natural healing when differentiating between the nine Gifts of the Spirit. They are not one and the same. A lot of people try to explain away Divine Healing by saying things like, "Medical doctors are healing instruments in God's hands." Yes, doctors can and are used frequently by God to heal His people but this system of man is in no way connected to the supernatural manifestation of the gifts of healings. If this where so, there should be no charge for medical services or procedures. Yes, medical doctors are used by God to bring "healing" in a measure to the masses, but if medical science is the only way God heals today, than what a broken system this would be with the thousands upon thousands currently dying of diseases throughout the world today. I have good news for you. Jesus Christ still freely heals today! When God heals, He heals completely. Praise The Lord for the Gifts of Supernatural Healings!

Now that we have established the gifts of healings are exclusively a supernatural intervention, let us look at a great example in the Word of God of these gifts at work in the tenth chapter of the Book of Acts:

Acts 10:38 *38 How God anointed Jesus of Nazareth with the Holy Ghost and with power: who went about doing good, and healing all that were oppressed of the devil; for God was with him*

Sickness and disease are from the devil. It is high time for the Church to be filled with God's word and power! So many churches that I have ministered in felt as though everyone in the meeting was sick. This should not be the case for a spirit filled Church. James Chapter Five says, *"Is any sick among you? let him call for the elders of the church; and let them pray over him, anointing him with oil in the name of the Lord:"*

Nowadays, in so many assemblies, I have felt like asking, "Is there any NOT sick among you?" Jesus paid too high of a price for His Church to be ridden with sickness and disease.

Isaiah 53:5 *But he was wounded for our transgressions, he was bruised for our iniquities: the chastisement of our peace was upon him; and with his stripes we are healed.*

Now, there are many ways to receive healing such as: by the anointing with oil, laying on of hands, hearing the word preached and taught or just simply receiving by faith in God's Written Word. There are so many examples of healing in the Bible, that if I were to put them all in this book, they would hardly fit.

I think it is important to note the fact that not only can anyone be healed by simply placing their faith in Jesus, but there is also a separate ministry given to the Church, through the nine Gifts of the Holy Spirit, known as "the gifts of healing". This specific gift can be found in the twelfth chapter of First Corinthians, the ninth verse:

1 Corinthians 12:9 *to another the gifts of healing by the same Spirit;*

This verse implies that there is separate ministry within the church, exclusive to the supernatural cure of the sick. With that having been stated, it also important to note verse thirty and thirty-one:

30 Have all the gifts of healing? do all speak with tongues? do all interpret? 31 But covet earnestly the best gifts:

The scripture implies that not everyone, at all times has this healing gift functioning in their life. This is then, a specific gift, supernatural from God, exclusively at work in the life of someone who has received the gifts of healing. I do not claim to understand how this exclusivity exists yet we clearly know from the Scriptures that it does. I believe, however, that anyone can operate in the gifts of healing as they "covet" or earnestly desire the best spiritual gift needed at the time. Distributing the Gifts of the Spirit is up to God, being available to be used is up to us. This brings me to another question someone might ask: Why then did Jesus say in Mark chapter 16 *"And these signs shall follow them that believe?"* The entire scripture reads: *17 And these signs shall follow them that believe; In my name shall they cast out devils; they shall speak with new tongues; 18 They shall take up serpents; and if they drink any deadly thing, it shall not hurt them; they shall lay hands on the sick, and they shall recover.*

Hallelujah, there is a simple answer! I believe that any believer in Christ, at anytime may lay hands on the sick and sickness has to go. This type of healing ministry is dependent mainly on the faith of the individuals involved. In short, you can receive healing by hearing the Word of God being taught, the laying on of hands etc. I believe that any form of "faith contact" will cause the healing anointing of Jesus to flow as long as you mix your hearing or doing with faith to receive. However, the first Corinthians chapter twelve Gifts of Healing are not as dependent upon the individuals faith, rather, are given or "divided" to individuals as the Spirit wills. Additionally, it is important to know that Jesus, while on the earth, had the Spirit without measure.

The Virtue Gifts

John 3:34 *For he whom God hath sent speaketh the words of God: for God giveth not the Spirit by measure unto him.*

Jesus had all of the gifts functioning within His ministry all of the time. This is why I believe it is so very important for the Church in the earth to come together. When we join in perfect unity, as "the Body of Christ," we can experience the Gifts of the Spirit just as Jesus did— "without measure."

Let us look at some of the different ways that the gifts of healing work together with the other nine Gifts of the Spirit. I will give a personal example:

Many times when I have conducted healing services, people with hearing problems will come to be cured. In my experience, I have noticed the word of knowledge in operation is important for me to correctly identify the individual needs of those I pray for. If I were to pray for someone's hearing to be restored, but I learn they do not have an eardrum, (requiring a creative miracle), the gift of the *working of miracles* would be required rather than the *gifts of healings* since there would be nothing to be healed because it physically never existed.

This is what Paul meant in 1 Corinthians 12:31 when he said, *"But covet earnestly the best gifts."* In other words, we are to earnestly desire or discern what is the best gift needed at the time and position ourselves to be available for God to use us in that way.

In this portion of scripture, the word *covet* is the Greek word ζηλόω transliterated as *zeloo*. It means *to be jealous of* or *eager to possess something*. It is of utmost importance that we yield ourselves to the leading of the Holy Spirit so we may be used in whatever gifts He so chooses to operate through our lives at any given time. No one person "has" or "owns" any of the spiritual gifts, this is why they are called the *gifts of the Spirit*. The Holy Spirit distributes the gifts; they are His to give. We should never say *"I have a gift"* or *"That person has a gift"* because by definition, they all belong to God! He is the giver of the gifts, and they function at *His* will, by *His* command.

1 Corinthians 12:11: *But all these worketh that one and the selfsame Spirit, dividing to every man severally* **as He will.**

It is of equal importance to learn that God's Spirit may allow us to function in multiple gifts at the same time. The gifts of the Spirit work in harmony with one another, each gift complementing another to help us help others.

For instance, the word of knowledge can work in conjunction with the discerning of spirits to better enable us to correctly identify a problem and its source. Although it is true that every sickness, malformity and disease are direct products of the curse brought upon all humanity because of Adam's fall; not every disease is immediately the result of a demon spirit. Therefore, sickness and disease are a direct product of the law of sin and death.

Romans 5:12: *Wherefore, as by one man sin entered into the world, and death by sin; and so death passed upon all men, for that all have sinned.*

This explains the reason that the final destination of sickness and disease, uncured, is ultimately death. However, every believer has been given a choice to live a life of freedom from the *"prison"* of sin and death because of the *second Adam's* (Christ Jesus') victory!

Romans 8:2-3: *For the law of the Spirit of life in Christ Jesus hath made me free from the law of sin and death.* 3*For what the law could not do, in that it* *was weak through the flesh, God sending his own Son in the likeness of sinful flesh, and for sin, condemned sin in the flesh:*

As believers we must begin to position ourselves into a place of perfect obedience and yieldedness so the Holy Spirit is able to divide unto us the appropriate gift for every individual situation. Too many times I have witnessed someone praying for another's healing when I knew, by the Spirit and through the gift of word of knowledge, a creative miracle was needed. If we are led by the Holy Spirit, we must learn to have the discernment to pray appropriately.

Another thing I have witnessed is individuals who come forward for prayer with a *spirit of infirmity* or *sickness*, while those praying did not discern the spiritual root of the problem. Every situation is completely different. In some instances, the sickness is caused by a demonic stronghold, but not every case is a direct result of demon oppression or possession. Furthermore, it is important to know that a Christian cannot be possessed by a demon spirit.

To be demon possessed is to be completely captivated — Spirit, Soul and Body. It is possible, however, for a demon spirit (or spirits) to "infest" a believer's body. This explains why so many believers live in pain and disease. Our spirit dwells in the house of our earthly body. Therefore, we must drive out any pestilence of sickness and disease through The Name of Jesus!

Throughout the years of pastoring several Churches, my wife and I have rented numerous houses, and some of them were over one hundred years old. Among the many things I have learned from moving into an old house, one stands out among the rest: *Before you stock the cabinets with food, always drive out the mice; otherwise, you'll be feeding them too!*

So many believers struggle to retain their healing or spiritual breakthrough simply because they have never "cleaned house." Demon spirits are like mice; they will devour everything you have if you allow them to stay. It is equally important to maintain your healing as it is to receive it. Never allow the enemy to steal anything from you that is rightfully yours. Keep your mind renewed by The Word of God and the devil will never rob you again! *Submit yourselves, then, to God. Resist the devil, and he will flee from you.* (James 4:7)

In order for us to maintain our rightful place we must be led by the Spirit of God and allow Him to divide the appropriate gift for the task at hand. The *gifts of healings* were vital to the life and ministry of Jesus and they are equally as important in the life of every believer today. Without the Father sending Jesus into the earth with His healing power, God would not have kept His promises prophesied throughout the Old Testament.

Psalm 107:20: *He sent his **word** and healed them and delivered them from their destructions.*

I believe the gifts of healing reveal the restorative nature of God. Jesus went to the Cross, not only to save us, but to heal us as well.

Isaiah 53:5: *But he was wounded for our transgressions, he was bruised for our iniquities: the chastisement of our peace was upon him; and by his stripes, we are healed.*——Healing is who Jesus is.

Ephesians 2:4-5: *But God, who is rich in mercy, for his great love wherewith he loved us, ⁵Even when we were dead in sins, hath quickened us together with Christ, (by grace ye are saved;)*

It is because of God's great love for us that the Father sent Jesus into the world to heal all of the brokenness and destruction caused by the darkness of sin.

John 11:10: *But if a man walks in the night, he stumbleth, because there is no light in him.*

Now more than ever, the Church of Jesus Christ needs to be functioning in the gifts of healings. It has been said, *"Actions speak louder than words."* It is great to preach a message of hope, but where is the hope if we cannot demonstrate what we have preached? Christ came to save that which is lost. It is one thing to do humanitarian work; to feed the hungry, clothe the naked; these things are needed in our world today. However, there are sick people who can be fed and clothed, but are left sick and dying.

In John 10:10 Jesus said, *"I have come that ye may have life, and life more abundantly."* I truly believe a person cannot live an abundant life and still be sick in their physical body.

In 2 Corinthians 3:17 we are told, *"Where the Spirit of the Lord is, there is liberty* (freedom)." Where Jesus is, sickness is *not.*

In John 8:36 Jesus declared *"...if the Son makes you free, you shall be free indeed."* In another passage Jesus stated: *"...ye shall know the truth and the truth shall make you free"* (John 8:32.)

Imagine what will happen when the Church, like Christ, in his humanity, visits the sick and brings healing to their physical bodies! Friend, nothing speaks louder than healing manifested. This was the secret to Jesus' ministry in the earth. If the gifts of healing functioned in Jesus' earthly life, so should they be flowing in the life of end-time believers!

First John 4:17 states, *"as he is, so are we in the earth."* Just as the Word carries the will of God and never returns void (Isaiah 55), so Jesus walked the earth in the power of the Spirit, healing all who were sick (Acts 10:38). Jesus gave substance to the will of the Father. We must, as the Church, function in the gifts of healings, demonstrating the "hands-on" healing nature of Jesus, the Living Word!

The Working of Miracles

The *working of miracles* is a very special category of the gifts of the Spirit. I pray the Holy Spirit sheds His light on the subject of this much needed spiritual gift.

Webster's Dictionary defines the word *miracle* as *an extraordinary event manifesting divine intervention in human affairs*. The Greek word for *miracle* in Strong's Concordance is τέρας or *teras* meaning *a wonder, portent, marvel*.

Because the word *miracle* is so loosely thrown around in our society today, I feel the true impact of the meaning has been lost concerning what an actual miracle looks like and how it affects a situation and the people around it.

In his book *Gifts of the Spirit* Kenneth E. Hagin writes, "As with many words in the English language, when we use the word *'miracle,'* it means one thing generally speaking, but used specifically it means something else. Sometimes the word *'miracle'* is used as a figure of speech. We talk about *'miracle* fabrics,' *'miracle* drugs,' and *'miracle* detergents.' None of these things is a *miracle* specifically speaking, but generally speaking, they are." In the general use of the word *miracle*, each one of the Gifts of the Spirit could be defined as a *miracle*. However, specifically speaking they are not considered a true miracle.

The *working of miracles*, then, is a specific act, such as Elisha's dividing a river by the sweep of a mantle (2 Kings 2:9-14).

In reality, the gift of the *working of miracles* is simply God demonstrating His divine will through *intervening in* or *disrupting the regular order of creation*. If there ever was a time the demonstration of God's power is needed in the earth, it is now. With so many people not believing in the existence of God, we as the Church have a prime opportunity to demonstrate the power and might of the God we serve through the gift of the *working of miracles*.

I want to examine some examples of the working of miracles found in both the Old and New Testaments.

Joshua 10:12-14: *Then spake Joshua to the Lord in the day when the Lord delivered up the Amorites before the children of Israel, and he said in the sight of Israel, Sun, stand thou still upon Gibeon; and thou, Moon, in the valley of Ajalon.* ¹³*And the sun stood still, and the moon stayed until the people had avenged themselves upon their enemies. Is not this written in the book of Jasher? So the sun stood still in the midst of heaven and hasted not to go down about a whole day.* ¹⁴*And there was no day like that before it or after it, that the Lord hearkened unto the voice of a man: for the Lord fought for Israel.*

The gift of the *working of miracles* is God interrupting the natural course of nature by His divine power because it is from His own power that all things were created. By the power of God, Joshua was able to speak a command to the sun and the solar system stood still! If God created the heavens, He can certainly rearrange or interrupt things in this natural realm. As Hebrews 1:3 says, *"all things are upheld by the word of His power."* The book of John provides an excellent account of the *working of miracles.*

John 2:1-11: *And the third day there was a marriage in Cana of Galilee, and the mother of Jesus was there: ²And both Jesus was called, and his disciples, to the marriage. ³And when they wanted wine, the mother of Jesus saith unto him, They have no wine. ⁴Jesus saith unto her, Woman, what have I to do with thee? mine hour is not yet come. ⁵His mother saith unto the servants, Whatsoever he saith unto you, do it. ⁶And there were set there six waterpots of stone, after the manner of the purifying of the Jews, containing two or three firkins apiece. ⁷Jesus saith unto them, Fill the waterpots with water. And they filled them up to the brim. ⁸And he saith unto them, Draw out now and bear unto the governor of the feast. And they bare it. **9**When the ruler of the feast had tasted the water that was made wine and knew not whence it was: (but the servants which drew the water knew;) the governor of the feast called the bridegroom, ¹⁰And saith unto him, Every man at the beginning doth set forth good wine; and when men have well drunk, then that which is worse: but thou hast kept the good wine until now. ¹¹This beginning of miracles did Jesus in Cana of Galilee and manifested forth his glory, and his disciples believed on him.*

Through the power of the Holy Spirit and by the gift of the *working of miracles,* Jesus was able to speak a word, change the molecular structure of a natural substance, and turn water into wine. Jesus' ministry was thrust into full throttle through the *working of miracles* as noted in the last part of verse eleven: *...and his disciples believed on him.*

The singular purpose of the gifts of the Spirit is that Jesus would be glorified. As previously stated, a *miracle* is *a divine disruption in the natural order of events.* Hallelujah! We must begin to open ourselves up to the leading of the Holy Spirit. He desires to manifest the *working of miracles* through His Church and distribute the gifts according to His will.

The Bible is filled with accounts of miracles, but the first and most important of these is recorded in Genesis 1:1: *In the beginning, God created the heavens and the earth.* If we believe this account of creation, it shouldn't be difficult to believe the rest of God's Word! Again, we must allow the Holy Spirit to demonstrate His miracle-working power through the gift of *working of miracles*; this gift demonstrates who Christ is in us and directly expresses the tangible, miraculous nature of Jesus, the Living Word!

The Gift of Faith

To conclude this study on the *Virtue Gifts* or *Power Gifts*, I believe the greatest of this category of gifts is the *gift of faith*. In Strong's Concordance, the word *faith* is πίστις, εως, ἡ or *pistis*. Strong's defines faith as *belief, trust, confidence; fidelity, faithfulness.*

In my opinion, there is no better definition of the word *faith* than described in the eleventh chapter of Hebrews:

Hebrews 11:1: *Now faith is the substance of the things hoped for; the evidence of things not seen.*

The *gift of faith* is a vitally important aspect of who God is.

Hebrews 11:3: *Through faith we understand that the worlds were framed by the word of God so that things which are seen were not made of things which do appear.*

My definition of the gift of *special faith*, as it has been called, is *an exchange of faith between a man and God.* This gift enables the working of miracles to function. As mentioned previously in this book, there are instances in which two or even three gifts of the Spirit may work together. It is important to note the difference between the *gift of faith* and the *working of miracles.* The *gift of faith* has nothing to do with us *"working"* anything. The *gift of faith* is God directly working through an individual, independent of their own faith.

Each of the three categories of the gifts of the Spirit are very closely related. Often, the *word of knowledge* will work in conjunction with the *word of wisdom.* God will frequently reveal His omniscience on a matter and then give us His wisdom on how to deal with a particular situation.

A great example of this truth is found in Luke chapter eleven.

Luke 11:9-13: *And I say unto you, Ask, **and it shall be given you**; seek, and ye shall find; knock, and it shall be opened unto you. For every one that asketh receiveth; and he that seeketh findeth, and to him that knocketh it shall be opened. If a son shall ask bread of any of you that is a father, will he give him a stone? Or if he asks a fish, will he for a fish give him a serpent? Or if he shall ask an egg, will he offer him a scorpion? If ye then, being evil, know how to **give good gifts** unto your children: **how much more** shall your **heavenly Father give the Holy Spirit to them that ask him**?*

Do you see a pattern here? *Seek and find; knock and the door shall be opened.* When the *word of wisdom* is in operation, you will have God's mind on *how* to *seek* an answer on a situation and through the *word of knowledge* *"find"* the answer needed.

Jeremiah 33:3: *Call unto me, and I will answer thee, and shew thee great and mighty things, which thou knowest not.*

God will never reveal a problem without providing a solution. He is faithful to complete that which He has begun in us.

Philippians 1:6: *Being confident of this very thing, that he which hath begun a good work in you will perform it until the day of Jesus Christ.*

The act of raising someone from the dead requires the *gift of faith.* Typically, the Gifts of the Spirit work together to manifest a response or solution to a problem. For example, the raising of the dead requires supernatural faith; not the faith that comes by hearing or the faith of agreement.

Matthew 18:18-19: *Verily I say unto you, Whatsoever ye shall bind on earth shall be bound in heaven: and whatsoever ye shall loose on earth shall be loosed in heaven. ¹⁹Again I say unto you, That if two of you shall agree on earth as touching anything that they shall ask, it shall be done for them of my Father which is in heaven.*

This kind of *special faith* is God's faith in operation through a yielded individual. The *working of miracles* is necessary to raise the person from the dead, but it also takes the *gifts of healings* in operation to bring about a cure for whatever was the initial cause of death; without the healing the individual would immediately die again.

John records a biblical example of this is in the account of Jesus raising Lazarus from the dead. Not only was Lazarus raised to life, he was also healed of the sickness responsible for his death.

John 11:1: *Now a certain man was sick, named Lazarus, of Bethany, the town of Mary and her sister Martha.*

The *gift of faith* seems to function often within the *Virtue Gifts*. As seen throughout the scriptures, the *gift of faith* will frequently accompany *the gift of the working of miracles.* It is also important to note that not all faith is of the same kind. I have come to believe there are three main types of faith available to every believer.

1) Salvation Faith: *faith given to you and me by God bringing us to salvation.*

Hebrews 11:6: *But without faith it is impossible to please him: for **he that cometh to God must believe** that he is and that he is a rewarder of them that diligently seek him. He that comes to God must believe.* This is saving faith at work.

2) Ever-Increasing Faith or **General Faith**: *the measure of faith given to every man after salvation, which can be increased or remain the same according to the gift of Christ at work in us.*

Romans 12:3: *For I say, through the grace given unto me, to every man that is among you, not to think of himself more highly than he ought to think; but to think soberly, according to as God hath dealt with every man the measure of faith.* This type of faith is also according to *how we hear the Word.*

Romans 10:17: *Now faith cometh by hearing, and hearing by the Word of God.*

In Romans 12:4 Paul says, *"For as we have many members in one body, and all members have not the same office: [5]So we, being many, are one body in Christ, and every one members one of another.[6]Having then gifts differing according to the grace that is given to us, whether prophecy, let us prophesy according to the proportion of faith."*

We see that every believer has a different *measure* of *General Faith* according to the gift of Christ at work in him and the faithfulness of the believer to hear the Word of God and do it.

James 2:17: *Even so Faith, if it hath not works, is dead, being alone.* Works are the body that gives our faith life and mobility.

James 2:26: *For as the body without the spirit is dead, so faith without works is dead also.*

3) The Gift of Faith: This is not your faith or my faith in action; but *God's very own faith given to us on loan. It is God's own, separate faith imparted into an individual for empowerment beyond their current level of believing.*

Hallelujah! We can have the very faith of God as His Spirit wills to divide or distribute to us. The *Gift of Faith*, when in operation, causes our words to literally become the very words of God. The *Gift of Faith* does not require the individual's faith because God is allowing us to share His faith. This is the realm where all things suddenly become possible.

Matthew 19:26: *But Jesus beheld them, and said unto them, With men this is impossible, but with God all things are possible.*

In concluding this study of the *Gift of Faith* and how it functions, it is important to note that these *Virtue Gifts* of the Spirit contain the very attributes of God, the Son.

1 Corinthians 12:8-9: *For to one is given by the Spirit the word of wisdom; to* *another the word of knowledge by the same Spirit;* 9**To another faith** *by the same Spirit; to another the gifts of healing by the same Spirit.*

When the Holy Spirit imparts the gift of faith to someone, the attribute of Jesus Christ's creative power is expressed. As John 1:3 declares, *"All things were made by him, and without him was not anything made that was made."*

When the Church begins to function in the supernatural manifestation of the *Gift of Faith*, signs, wonders, and miracles will become a normal way of life for the believer. This way of living will ultimately exalt Christ, in His power, before the eyes of the world.

As stated earlier in this study, no one individual has a gift unless it is given to him by the Holy Spirit. It is not us but God working through us by His Spirit.

Philippians 2:13: *For it is God which worketh in you both to will and to do of his good pleasure.*

Let us never fall into the trap of pride, but be diligent God chasers knowing that *every good and perfect gift comes from above* (James 1:17). If any man had the ability in himself to conjure up the gifts of the Spirit, it would not be of God.

In conclusion, *the Gift of Faith* manifests Jesus, the Living Word, in all of His limitless power! Colossians 1:17 states, *"By Him all things consist* (were created) *and do hold together."* The gift of faith directly expresses the omnipotent nature Jesus Christ, the Word, in His fullness.

CHAPTER SIX
The Vocal Gifts

We will now examine the final category of the gifts of the Spirit, the mighty third Person of the Trinity revealed through the function of the Vocal Gifts.

I have arranged the *Vocal Gifts* into three main categories: *The Gift of Prophecy, The Gift of Tongues,* and *The Gift of the Interpretation of Tongues.*

In the modern Church, I believe there is no subject more shrouded in ignorance than the subject of the Vocal Gifts of the Spirit, and especially *tongues* and *the interpretation of tongues.* The *utterance gifts* or *the Vocal Gifts* have one predominant purpose: *They relay what is the mind, will, and purpose of God to the Church who are on the earth.*

Each one of the *Vocal Gifts* function to exhort, edify, and comfort the Body of Christ.

1 Corinthians 14:13: *But he that prophesieth speaketh unto men to edification, and exhortation, and comfort.*

The *Vocal Gifts* all work together to accomplish the twofold task of *building up the Body of Christ* and demonstrate the speaking qualities of God to the world through the sign of *tongues, interpretation of tongues,* and *prophecy.* These *Vocal Gifts* function directly through the ministry of the Holy Spirit and are of great importance during man's temporary time on earth. **1 Corinthians 13:8:** *Charity never faileth: but whether there be prophecies, they shall fail; whether there be tongues, they shall cease; whether there be knowledge, it shall vanish away.*

The Vocal Gifts of the Spirit must be yielded to in our daily lives and our churches. Without the essential functioning of the Vocal Gifts, God cannot speak to the masses concerning His Redemptive plan for man. Yes, the world has been given the Bible, the written Word of God; still, so many people do not read what He says in His Word, which is one of the many reasons for the need of the operation of the vocal gifts in the Church and the world.

Thank God for these *Vocal Gifts* of the Spirit functioning in the Church today through the *gift of prophecy*, the *gift of tongues* and *the interpretation of tongues*. Many people argue that the *Vocal Gifts* of the Spirit have passed away, but we know, through the Word of God that this is untrue. All of the Gifts of the Spirit are in operation today waiting for us to yield to the power of the Holy Spirit who dwells within us! If even one of the gifts have disappeared or expired, then all of the other gifts have ceased. But the gifts of the Spirit are still in operation today. Many people who refuse the *gift of tongues* still choose to believe in healing. This is most ironic. Thank God none of the gifts are passed away! As long as the Holy Spirit is on the earth, His nine gifts will most definitely function!

Acts 2:39: *For the promise is unto you, and to your children, and to all that are afar off, even as many as the Lord our God shall call.*

Thank God that the same Holy Spirit received by believers at the inception of the Church, is the same Holy Spirit that will sustain the end-time Church. It seems that whenever I minister on the gifts of the Spirit, especially the *gift of tongues* and the *interpretation of tongues*, I spend time after the service with a few spiritually uneducated individuals concerning the New Testament gifts of the Spirit, who try to convince me and themselves that the Gifts of the Spirit have passed away.

I will simply ask them one question: *Are you God-called?* Usually, without reservation, the response is an unabashedly resounding YES; *Of course I am called by God!* I will then ask them to read Acts 2:39, which says, *For the promise* (the gift of the Holy Spirit) *is unto you, and to your children, and to all that are afar off, even as many as the LORD our God shall call.* Without fail, when they arrive at the part in the verse where the Apostle Peter proclaims *...and to all that are afar off,* **even as many as the Lord our God shall call,** I proceed to ask them if they believe God has called them. To their utter shock and amazement, they answer "Well, yes. I am called that's me! Hallelujah!" If you can be saved, you can be Spirit-filled! One of my greatest joys in life has been seeing people receive the wonderful Baptism in the Holy Spirit with the evidence of speaking in tongues. Suddenly, what they had so vehemently questioned is confirmed.

Friend, you cannot deny something you have never experienced. Applesauce is okay, but once I had steak my idea of a good meal changed forever! Proverbs 18:13 wisely declares: *He that answereth a matter before he heareth it, it is folly and shame unto him.* Do not ever allow something you don't know to keep you from something you *can* know! It is foolish for those who deny the *gift of tongues* and who have never spoken in tongues, to refute its existence. I have never met an individual who has received the gift of the Holy Spirit, deny it.

Hallelujah! There are nine gifts of the Spirit mentioned in 1 Corinthians 12, and all of these gifts are given to us for today!

Isaiah 28:11-12: *For with stammering lips and another tongue will he speak to this people* [12]*To whom he said, This is the rest wherewith ye may cause the weary to rest, and this is the refreshing: yet they would not hear.*

The *Vocal Gifts* of the Spirit are a direct expression of God, the Holy Spirit's voice to the world. Are you yielded and listening? Are you ready to be Gods' mouthpiece in the earth?

I want to delve into the Vocal Gifts of the Spirit to increase our understanding of their purpose and how they function within body of Christ.

Vocal Gifts: *Tongues, The interpretation of Tongues* and *the Gift of Prophecy* = **Holy Spirit**

The Gift of Tongues

In my opinion, the *gift of tongues* is the least understood manifestation of the Spirit and for many is seemingly shrouded in mystery. The Apostle Paul wrote an entire chapter on this one gift alone in 1 Corinthians Chapter 14. The *gift of tongues* can be separated into two distinct categories: *tongues of men* and *tongues of angels*.

1 Corinthians 13:1: *Though I speak with the tongues of men and of angels, and have not charity, I have become as sounding brass, or a tinkling cymbal.*

There are over 6,500 unique and diverse known languages in the earth today. However, approximately 2,000 of those known languages have fewer than 1,000 individuals who speak those languages. At the time of this writing, the most spoken language in the world is Mandarin Chinese with over 1,213,000,000 people who speak Mandarin.

To gain a better understanding of the origins of language and the power it contains, the account of the Tower of Babel provides great insights.

Genesis 11:1-9: *And the whole earth was of one language, and of one speech. ²And it came to pass, as they journeyed from the east, that they found a plain in the land of Shinar; and they dwelt there. ³And they said one to another, Go to, let us make brick, and burn them thoroughly. And they had brick for stone, and slime had them for mortar. ⁴And they said, Go to, let us build us a city and a tower,*
whose top may reach unto heaven; and let us make us a name, lest we are scattered abroad upon the face of the whole earth. ⁵And the Lord came down to see the city and the tower, which the children of men built. ⁶And the Lord said, Behold, the people is one, and they have all one language; and this they begin to do: and now nothing will be restrained from them, which they have imagined doing. ⁷Go to, let us go down, and there confound their language, that they may not understand one another's speech. ⁸So the Lord scattered them abroad from thence upon the face of all the earth: and they left off to build the city. ⁹Therefore is the name of it called

Babel; because the Lord did there confound the language of all the earth: and from thence did the Lord scatter them abroad upon the face of all the earth.

Verse four indicates that the desire of the people at this time was to build a tower reaching to the heavens. Many Bible scholars have suggested that the people of the earth desired to do so because they were attempting to build a monument of worship to the heavens and gain solicited knowledge through the study of the stars. Oxford Dictionary of English states: *"Astrology is the study of the movements and relative positions of celestial objects as a means of divining information about human affairs and terrestrial events."*

I am thoroughly convinced that this is the reason God came to earth and disrupted humanity's agenda.

Genesis 11:6-7: *And the Lord said, Behold, the people is one, and they have all one language; and this they begin to do: and now nothing will be restrained from them, which they have **imagined** doing. 7Go to, let us go down, and there confound their language, that they may not understand one another's speech.* Notice the word *imagine*. The Hebrew word for *imagine*, found in Strong's Concordance, is הָתַת or *hathath* meaning *to imagine mischief*. Note the word *understand* in verse 7. The Hebrew word for *understand* in Strong's Concordance is שָׁמַע, translated *shama*, meaning *to hear*. Language is vital to God and to humanity; without it we are incapable of understanding each other or God! I believe this is the reason the gift of *speaking in tongues* has been so strongly opposed by the devil; he knows when believers have a revelation of the great importance of speaking in other tongues—speaking the language of God—the Church will be unstoppable in the realm of the Spirit! The *gift of tongues* is vital to the life of every Spirit-filled believer. This gift is our divine connection with the throne of God. In 1 Corinthians 14:14 Paul said, *"For if I pray in an unknown tongue, my spirit prayeth, but my understanding is unfruitful."*

When we are living a Spirit-led life by praying in other tongues both in the languages of men unknown to us and in the languages of angels, also unknown to us, our spirit is praying to God in a language God can understand even if we don't! This is the reason Paul makes the statement: *My understanding is unfruitful.*

The word *understanding* in this verse is the Greek word νοῦς, transliterated as *nous,* phonetically spelled *nooce.* It means *mind, understanding, reason* or *intellect.* You and I are limited by the things we *do not know* and consequentially suffer and perish because of it.

Hosea 4:6: *My people are destroyed for lack of knowledge: because thou hast rejected knowledge.*

As humanity, we are confined to two realms of time: *the past* and *the present.* Our human experience is limited to these two planes. However, God is the One who was and is and is to come! He knows the future from the past and all that lies in between.

Revelation 1:8: *I am Alpha and Omega, the beginning and the ending, saith the Lord, which is, and which was, and which is to come.*

When our spirits pray in an unknown tongue, God's perfect will is prayed out on the earth. We are able to pray from God's standpoint on any situation. This is the reason the *gift of tongues* is so desperately needed in the Church today and I believe the reason the devil has tried so adamantly to snuff-out this most essential gift in the body of Christ.

Another reason the *gift of tongues* is vital to believers today is because it is the avenue God has provided for us to be built up and strengthened for the opposition of the enemy of our souls.

Jude 1:20: *But ye, beloved, building up yourselves on your most holy faith, praying in the Holy Ghost.*

When we pray in the Spirit with unknown tongues, *we speak not unto men but unto God.*

1 Corinthians 14:2: *For he that speaketh in an unknown tongue speaketh not unto men, but unto God: for no man understandeth him; howbeit in the Spirit he speaketh **mysteries**.*

Hallelujah! What a magnificent, limitless gift we have been given! According to Strong's Concordance, the word *mysteries* found in this passage is the Greek word μυστήριον, ου, τό or *muste'rion* meaning *a mystery, secret, of which initiation is necessary; in the NT: the counsels of God, once hidden but now revealed in the Gospel or some fact thereof; the Christian revelation generally; particular truths or details of the Christian revelation.*

In other words, when you and I pray in spiritual tongues, we are causing things that were hidden in the mind of God to be revealed to us in the earth! What a faith revelation! What a holy illumination of truth! This is the very reason the *gift of tongues* is so vital to our everyday Christian walk. A life of praying in the Spirit is a life lived before the throne of God. You and I never-need to view the future as dark and unknown. Instead, if we pray in the Spirit we have access and can know the mind and will of God Himself!

Romans 8:26: *Likewise the Spirit also helpeth our infirmities: for we know not what we should pray for as we ought: but the Spirit itself maketh intercession for us with groanings which cannot be uttered.*

As the Apostle Paul states in this verse of scripture; with mere human knowledge we do not know what we should pray for. However, the Holy Spirit, who lives on the inside of us, knows everything before we ask. After all, that is His job!

John 16:13: *Howbeit when he, the Spirit of truth, is come, he will guide you into all truth: for he shall not speak of himself; but whatsoever he shall hear, that shall he speak: and he will shew you things to come.*

When we pray in other tongues daily, we will see the plan of God manifested in and through our lives. Praying in the Spirit can be defined as, *"God's Spirit praying through our human spirit the answer for tomorrow's needs."* The greatest way to assure God's plan is fulfilled in our lives is by praying in other tongues, praying in the Spirit. There are two types of tongues described in the Bible: 1) *Personal Tongues*—the tongues of the believer's initial infilling.

2) *Diverse Tongues*—one of the spiritual gifts described in 1 Corinthians 12: 10. Personal tongues received is the foremost sign or evidence of the Holy Spirit's filling or overflow (baptism) at the time of the initial infilling of a believer as recorded in the Book of Acts. In other words, *Salvation is when the Holy Spirit comes in; Holy Ghost baptism is when He fills you so fully that He overflows out!*

Acts 2:1-4: *And when the day of Pentecost has fully come, they were all with one accord in one place. ²And suddenly there came a sound from heaven as of a rushing mighty wind, and it filled all the house where they were sitting. ³And there appeared unto them cloven tongues like as of fire, and it sat upon each of them. ⁴And they were all filled with the Holy Ghost and began to speak with other tongues, as the Spirit gave them utterance.*

From the time of this initial outpouring of the Holy Spirit on the day of Pentecost, the *gift of tongues* is the evidence of His overflowing, indwelling presence as repeatedly recorded in the Bible.

Acts 2:5-11: *And there were dwelling at Jerusalem Jews, devout men, out of every nation under heaven. ⁶Now when this was noised abroad, the multitude came together and was confounded, because that every man heard them speak in his own language. ⁷And they were all amazed and marveled, saying one to another, Behold, are not all these which speak Galilaeans? ⁸And how hear we every man in our own tongue, wherein we were born? ⁹Parthians, and Medes, and Elamites, and the dwellers in Mesopotamia, and in Judaea, and Cappadocia, in Pontus, and Asia, ¹⁰Phrygia, and Pamphylia, in Egypt, and in the parts of Libya* *about Cyrene, and strangers of Rome, Jews, and proselytes,* [11]*Cretes and Arabians,* **we do hear them speak in our tongues the wonderful works of God.**

Verse 10 describes a supernatural sign manifested in the streets of Jerusalem and heard by the devout international Jews who had traveled to Jerusalem to celebrate the festival of Pentecost. They heard uneducated Galilaeans speaking their native languages with perfect dialects declaring God's wonderful works! In this instance, those filled with the Holy Spirit on the Day of Pentecost not only received the initial *gift of tongues*, but they also spoke with *divers kinds of tongues.*

There have been many instances while ministering during a service, when I have begun praying in my personal prayer language in tongues when the tongues I am praying suddenly changes to one unfamiliar to me. When this happens, I normally wait on the Holy Spirit to give me an interpretation of these tongues in English. (We will discuss the gift of the interpretation of tongues in the next section).

Sometimes in these instances, I will begin to speak out the tongue publicly sensing the language shift from my "known" spirit tongue to an unknown sounding tongue. Many times these prayer languages that are unknown to me will be understood by others present in a service whose native language is not my own; those from around the world who speak languages unknown to me! To me a tongue may be unknown, but to those present the tongue might be known and in their native tongue. One day, I had a Jewish woman tell me that while I was praying in the Spirit, she overheard me speaking the words *"Father, I worship You"* over and over again in the Hebrew Language. This is a good example of an unknown tongue to the individual speaking or praying, being revealed by the Holy Spirit in the known tongue of someone else. The sole purpose for instances like this is for God to demonstrate compassion and power in the earth. Tongues is a supernatural utterance by the Holy Spirit in a language that has never been learned or understood by the speaker nor is understood by the intellect. Speaking with tongues has nothing whatsoever to do with linguistic capability. Speaking in other tongues has absolutely nothing to do with the mind of man; it is a "vocal miracle." We must understand that the *gift of tongues* is just that, *it is a gift*. Like all the other gifts of the Spirit, tongues is a very important gift, but is intended for use on a daily basis in the lives of believers who have received the gift. Never once will we read of Jesus, during His earthly ministry, while he was on this earth, speaking in spiritual tongues. Why? Because speaking in tongues is specific to the dispensation in which we are living; the *dispensation of the Church* or the *Church Age*, also called the *dispensation of grace*. The Church Age began in Acts chapter two on the day of Pentecost.

The gift of *diverse tongues* listed in 1 Corinthians 14, is a sign for unbelievers when it is followed by the gift of *interpretation of tongues*.

1 Corinthians 14:24-25: *But if all prophesy, and an unbeliever or an uninformed person comes in, he is convinced by all, he is convicted by all. ²⁵And thus are the secrets of his heart made manifest; and so falling down on his face he* *will worship God, and report that God is in you of a truth.* Tongues, when followed by an interpretation, is the equivalent of the *gift of prophecy.* This truth will be further explained in the next section.

Another reason for the prominence of tongues in the Church today is because tongues is a devotional or worship gift. Among the many uses for the *gift of tongues,* personal, spiritual edification is one of the most important. In 1 Corinthians 14:17-18 Paul says, *"For **thou verily givest thanks well**, but the other is not edified.[18] I thank my God, I speak with tongues more than ye all."* The Apostle Paul is saying that tongues, when used in our personal, private prayer life, is the most effective way we can magnify God.

Notice the words *thou givest thanks well.* Howard Carter, an English Pioneer of Pentecostalism known for his teaching on The Gifts of The Spirit said, *"We must not forget that the speaking with other tongues is not only an initial evidence of the Holy Spirit's indwelling, it is a continual stream that should never dry up, and that will enrich the life spiritually."* The *gift of tongues* is most vital in the life of every believer today; it is the secret key which unlocks the door for the gifts of the Spirit to function in one's life.

Most non-Spirit filled believers have one common argument against this spiritual gift. If I have heard it once, I have heard it a million times, *"Why do people speak in tongues in a public service?"* If tongues is not a teaching or preaching gift, why should it be exercised in the Church? Paul emphasized in 1 Corinthians 14:19, *"Yet in the church, I had rather speak five words with my understanding, that by my voice I might teach others also, than ten thousand words in an unknown tongue."* Paul was simply expressing the fact that speaking in tongues is good in a personal setting, but not beneficial in public unless followed by an interpretation in a known tongue.

Most of the time, if while I am preaching or ministering in a service and I sense the desire to pray in tongues, I will first discern whether it is a public tongue to be followed by an interpretation or if it is my personal, private prayer of worship. If I sense the Holy Spirit leading me to publicly utter this language of the Spirit, I will do so and after the utterance I will wait for the interpretation from the Holy Spirit either through me or someone else in the service.

God will never interrupt His Word by His Word. Rarely will a tongue or interpretation of tongues be heard while someone is ministering the Word from the pulpit in a public assembly.

To avoid confusion about what God is saying in a public assembly, it is good to allow only two or, at the most, three to speak out in tongues and interpret. In 1 Corinthians 14, The Apostle Paul teaches a general rule of thumb to permit a maximum of three people to give a tongue. The remaining time should be spent interpreting those messages into the "language of men" within a public meeting for the sake of decency and order.

1 Corinthians14:27-28: *If any man speaks in an unknown tongue, let it be by two, or at the most by three, and that by course; and let one interpret.* **28***But if there be no interpreter, let him keep silence in the church; and let him speak to* *himself, and to God.*

1 Corinthians 14:40: *Let all things be done decently and in order.*

How wonderful the gifts of the Spirit are when we are willing to yield to those gifts. As Smith Wigglesworth, a mighty Evangelist in the Pentecostal Movement, said, *"It is so important to not use the spirit of liberty, but allow the spirit of liberty to use us."*
In 1 Peter 2:16 we find a description and support for this quote: *As free, and not using your liberty for a cloak of maliciousness, but as the servants of God.*

We must purpose to begin praying in the Spirit daily and watch as God's plan unfolds in our lives. Remember, the Church Age is the only dispensation of time in which the gifts of the Spirit are necessary.

1 Corinthians 13:8: *Charity never faileth: but whether there be prophecies, they shall fail; whether there be* **tongues, they shall cease;**

Let us not neglect to pray in the Spirit, especially in these perilous times in which we live. It is a great gift that must be exercised to reap all of its spiritual benefits!

1 Corinthians 13:1: *Though I speak with the tongues of men and of angels, and have not charity, I have become as sounding brass or a tinkling cymbal.*

The *gift of tongues* is a vital, spiritual component in the life of every believer. It not only expresses the very language of God, but the will of God as well. **Matthew 16:17-18:** *And these signs shall follow them that believe; In my name* *shall they cast out devils;* **they shall speak with new tongues;**

The *gift of tongues* manifests the speaking attribute of the Holy Spirit through the Church. The *gift of tongues* transforms our human limitation of speech into the limitless ability to access the inexhaustible knowledge of God!

The Gift of the Interpretation of Tongues

The gift of *interpretation of tongues* is the only gift of the Spirit that cannot be a standalone gift. Because of this, it is the least of all of the other gifts of the Spirit. This specific gift can only function when the gift of tongues is in operation and, as the name implies, through this gift the Holy Spirit gives the interpretation of those tongues.

That being said, the gift of interpretation of tongues is a vitally important part of the vocal category of the gifts of the Spirit and it is equally important in the life of every Spirit-filled believer and Church. The specific purpose of this vocal gift is bringing the unknown (spiritual) tongue into a known (intellectual) tongue, relaying the mind and will of God to us.

Paul did not call this gift the *"translation"* of tongues; he called it the *"interpretation"* of tongues. The word *interpret* in the Webster's Dictionary is defined as *to explain or tell the meaning of to present in understandable terms; to conceive in the light of an individual belief, judgment, or circumstance.* The gift of the *interpretation of tongues* directly functions through the mind of the believer. In other words, the Holy Spirit relays the message of God to our human spirit, the human spirit relays the message to the mind, and the mind gives an interpretation of what God is communicating. I believe having this is what spiritual understanding really means. Praying in tongues is praying forth mysteries.

Romans 8:26: *Likewise the Spirit also helpeth our infirmities: for we know not what we should pray for as we ought: but the Spirit itself maketh intercession for us with groanings which cannot be uttered.*

I believe true spiritual understanding is gained through the process of praying in unknown tongues and the interpretation, pulling the spirit realm into the realm of the natural (understanding) causing what was unknown to become known or understood.

If every believer would practice this spiritual understanding in their individual prayer lives on a daily basis, I believe we would receive a clearer understanding of God's daily will for our lives. This gift is an interpretation or rendering of a spiritual message and is subject to the spiritual level or maturity of the believer through whom it is working. Countless times I have witnessed the gift of interpretation following an utterance in spiritual tongues. There are times some messages in tongues will be very lengthy and when the Holy Spirit gives the interpretation, an individual will only speak a few sentences. This does not mean the tongue or interpretation was inaccurate, but was simply an interpretation. It might take man a whole paragraph to speak what God can communicate in five words! I believe this fact alone, is another reason that the gift of the *interpretation of tongues* is such a supernatural gift.

The *gift of tongues* and the *interpretation of tongues* combined equal the gift of *prophecy*. This *gift of interpretation* is a wonderful gift useful for bringing edification to the life of every believer.

1 Corinthians 14:5: *I would that ye all spake with tongues, but rather that ye prophesied: for greater is he that prophesieth than he that speaketh with tongues, except he interprets, that the church may receive edifying.*

Through the believer, the *interpretation of tongues* expresses the nurturing vocal attribute of the Holy Spirit on a human level. Praise God for this interpretive gift!

The Gift of Prophecy

Although the *gift of prophecy* is the last gift of the Spirit we will explore, it is by no means the least of the nine manifestations of the gifts of the Spirit mentioned in First Corinthians: **1 Corinthians 12:10** *"to another prophecy;"*

Strong's Concordance defines the word *prophecy* as *the gift of communicating and enforcing revealed truth*. In other words, the *gift of prophecy* is God, the Holy Spirit's way of communicating His will to us concerning our lives. **1 Corinthians chapter 14:5:** *I would that ye all spake with tongues, but rather that ye prophesied: for greater is he that prophesieth than he that speaketh with tongues, except he interprets, that the church may receive edifying.*

This Scripture reveals that the *gift of tongues* and *interpretation of tongues* are equal to the one *gift of prophecy*. Prophecy is the greatest of the vocal gifts. The word *prophecy* is *an utterance* or, as Strong's Concordance defines the word, it means *to speak forth*.

Prophecy is *God speaking forth His Word to us concerning our world, the Church, governments, and our personal lives.*

The word *prophecy* in the *koine* or *biblical Greek* is προφητεία, ας, ἡ and is translated prophéteia, which is pronounced as *prof-ay-ti'-ah'*. The origin for the word *prophecy* comes from the old French word *profecie*, which is directly descended from the late Latin word *profecia*, which was derived from the *koine* Greek word, *prophetia*.

This word *prophetia* consists of two, separate Greek words, *pró*, meaning *before* and *phēmí*, meaning *to say or declare*. Strictly speaking, prophecy deals with the present and future. In short, Prophecy means to "utter-before".

It is important to understand that every prophecy that is legitimately from God will always bear witness with what is recorded in His Word.

As 1 Corinthians 14:29 declares, *"Let the prophets speak two or three, and let the other judge."* In other words, let every word of prophecy spoken be judged according to the standard of the Word of God. If you are given a prophecy and it does not bear witness with your spirit or measure up to the Bible, throw it out! I believe we should weigh prophesies against a minimum of two or three Scriptures.

1 Corinthians 13:1: *In the mouth of two or three witnesses shall every word be established.*

I believe it is important in guarding our hearts against error, that every message or word labeled *prophecy* be spoken publicly.

2 Peter 1:20: *Knowing this first, that no prophecy of the scripture is of any private interpretation.*

When prophecy is given in a public setting, it can be judged or tested against the Word of God and by spiritually discerning saints who flow in the prophetic. Every gift of the Spirit will have a single focus of pointing man back to Christ.

1 John 4:1-2: *Beloved, believe not every spirit, but try the spirits whether they are of God: because many false prophets are gone out into the world. Hereby know ye the Spirit of God: Every spirit that confesseth that Jesus Christ has come in the flesh is of God:*

Any real word of prophecy can be trusted as long as it exalts Jesus and bears witness with the Word of God. Over the years I have observed a common misunderstanding I feel needs to be addressed. Many times people confuse the *word of wisdom* and *word of knowledge* (visual or revelation gifts) with *prophecy* (a vocal gift) believing these gifts to be the same. However, these three gifts of the Spirit are *not* one and the same.

First, the *word of wisdom* deals expressly with God's mind concerning a matter. The *word of knowledge* deals with God's mind on *understanding* a matter, and the gift of *prophecy* expresses what God has to say or speak about the matter.

Prophecy is God vocalizing His will concerning a situation. It is important to note that many times, when the gift of prophecy is in operation, the *word of wisdom* and/or the *word of knowledge* will also be functioning.

We are exhorted in 1 Corinthians 14:1 to, "*Follow after charity, and desire spiritual gifts, but rather that ye may prophesy.*" I believe it is imperative that we, as the Church, should position our hearts into a place where the Lord, through the Holy Spirit, may divide to us the gift of *prophecy*.

Many people in our society today are in need of answers for many problems and a seemingly bleak future, but I am certain that the Church has the solutions by the agency of the Holy Spirit and His gifts! It is high time for the Church to have a "*thus sayeth the Lord*" answer! There are certain seasons when it may seem that God is not speaking through His gifts today, I am here to tell you that He has and He is! Hallelujah! God never changes! Hebrews 12:8 states *Jesus Christ the same yesterday, and today, and forever.*

It seems many in the modern day Church have become ignorant and, in some cases, frightened of the manifestations of the Spirit. However, there is a remnant of people the Lord has reserved for this time. I believe this *remnant* will literally speak as the oracles of God.

Samuel the prophet described the spiritual climate of his day when he said, "*And the word of the LORD was precious in those days; there was no open vision*" (1 Samuel 3:1). In the Hebrew Bible, this word *precious* means *rare* or *costly*. Some may relate to this today but God is not finished with His Church! This is the season to encourage. I implore you today to stop looking at others God is using and realize He desires to speak through you! Being in a five-fold ministry office (Ephesians 4:11-13), is not required for the operation of the gifts of the Spirit through the Church today! It is high time for the body of Christ to awaken from spiritual slumber and to earnestly pursue and receive the gifts of the Spirit, which were freely given to us by Jesus Christ over 2,000years ago!

Isaiah 60:1: *Arise, shine; for thy light is come, and the glory of the Lord has risen upon thee!*

It is important to note that during the time of the Old Testament only three groups of people were anointed to prophesy: *the king, the priest,* and *the prophet.* The time of the Old Covenant was prior to the dispensation of grace and the finished work of the Cross. Examples of the prophetic in operation in the Old Testament are profuse and too numerous to explore in this book.

Psalm 68:18 had not yet been fulfilled: *Thou hast ascended on high, thou hast led captivity captive: thou hast received gifts for men; yea, for the rebellious also, that the LORD God might dwell among them.* This time period was before the Holy Spirit was given to everyone who receives Him in His fullness, because Jesus had not yet come; He had not yet *led captivity captive.* He had not yet *ascended on high* and had not yet sent the Comforter, the Spirit of truth.

Acts 2:38: *Then Peter said unto them, Repent, and be baptized every one of you in the name of Jesus Christ for the remission of sins, and* **ye shall receive the gift of the Holy Ghost**.

On this very day, the Holy Ghost was given for the entire world to receive in order to be partakers of the *gifts of the Spirit.* The book of 1 Corinthians supports the fact that the gift of prophecy will work through any man or women who will yield to that gift.

1 Corinthians 14:38-39: **If any man** *thinks himself to be a prophet, or spiritual, let him acknowledge that the things that I write unto you are the commandments of the Lord. Wherefore, brethren, covet to prophesy and forbid not to speak with tongues.*

The Apostle Paul gives a very distinct command in this portion of scripture: Any man (or woman) who desires to prophesy, may do so freely. Brothers and sisters, my desire is that you will be enlightened about the availability of the Gifts of the Spirit to anyone who will simply yearn to possess them.

Joel 2:28-29: *And it shall come to pass afterward, that I will pour out my Spirit upon all flesh; and* **your sons and your daughters shall prophesy,** *your old men shall dream dreams, your young men shall see visions:* ²⁹ *And also upon the servants and upon the handmaids in those days will I pour out my Spirit.*

Conclusion

My earnest desire is that through the pages of this book, you may have caught a glimpse into what is available to you as a child of God. However, the question remains, *are you available to God?* The gifts of the Spirit are yours for the taking, accessible to anyone who will dare to possess them. I believe the very purpose behind the nine gifts of the Spirit is to manifest the Holy Trinity through revealing their individual attributes to the world.

Furthermore, I believe the nine gifts of the Spirit are literally God's expression of Himself through the Church, the Body of Christ. If we, as New Testament, believers will yield ourselves to the working of God's mighty Spirit, we will become living and authentic demonstrations of the *Father*, the *Son*, and the *Holy Spirit*.

As we have learned, each of the three members in the Godhead are separate personalities, exemplifying individual manifestations exclusive to their nature. You and I have seen this fact demonstrated in detail through the three categories of the gifts of the Spirit: the *Visual Gifts, Virtue Gifts,* and *Vocal Gifts.*

The *Visual Gifts* demonstrates the omniscient wisdom, knowledge, and discernment of the Father on His eternal throne as He sends forth His creative Word, which has formed all things past, present and future.

Through the *Virtue Gifts,* we have clearly seen Jesus, the Living Word, in all of His mighty power, sent into the earth, tangibly demonstrating the love of the Father. Jesus Christ proceeded from the Father God and is the Living, creative Word, which formed the earth from nothing and Adam from the dust.

While on the earth, Jesus was the hands and feet of the will of God the Father. And today, the body of Christ has become those very same hands and feet of Jesus; *healing the sick, raising the dead, casting out devils* while demonstrating the same signs, wonders, and miracles that flowed through Jesus, for the world to see and believe. It is through these virtue *gifts of healings, the working of miracles*, and the *gift of faith* that Christ Jesus can literally be touched through the body of Christ!

Hebrews 12:2: *Looking unto Jesus the author and finisher of our faith; who for the joy that was set before him endured the cross, despising the shame, and is set down at the right hand of the throne of God.*

Finally, we have learned the vital role the Holy Spirit fulfills through His Church in these last days. He is the very One through whom the voice of God is heard. It is through the Holy Spirit's power that the speaking attribute of *Yahweh Elohim*, God in three Persons, is revealed. I believe they are revealed through the vocal gifts of the Spirit, which are the *gift of diverse tongues, interpretation of tongues*, and the *gift of prophecy*. These three *Vocal Gifts* are the guiding voice for the Church today, uttering the mind, will, and emotions of God through the body of Christ.

I believe these nine gifts of the Spirit, when functioning in perfect harmony together throughout the end-time body, will be the fulfillment of Ephesians 4:13: *Till we all come in the unity of the faith, and of the knowledge of the Son of God, unto a perfect man, unto the measure of the stature of the fulness of Christ.* This perfect unity will testify to Heaven that the Bride of Christ is perfect and complete and the fields of earth have been thoroughly harvested. God will look at His Creation, His Body, beholding the divine order set into motion through the nine gifts of the

Spirit. I believe this will mark the beginning of the end; this will be when Jesus cries out, *"Come up hither, it is finished, I call it Good (Tov)."*

And when these things begin to come to pass, then look up, and lift up your heads; for your redemption draweth nigh. **Luke 21:28**

Revelation 4:1:*After this I looked, and, behold, a door was opened in heaven: and the first voice which I heard was as it were of a trumpet talking with me; which said,* **Come up hither,** *and I will shew thee things which must be hereafter.*

God desires to express Himself through YOU, will you answer the call?

Has anyone ever told you that God has a plan for your life? **I**f you were to die today, where would you spend eternity? **I**f you would like to receive the gift of Salvation and know without a doubt that Heaven is your final destination, pray this prayer:

Dear Lord Jesus, come into my heart. Forgive me of my sins. Wash me in Your blood. Set me free. Jesus, thank You that You died for me. I believe that You are risen from the dead and that you are coming back again for me. Fill me with the Holy Spirit. I believe that I am saved. I am now born again. I am forgiven and I am on my way to Heaven because Jesus now lives in me.

If you prayed that prayer you are Born Again! It is now your duty to share this good news with everyone around you so that they might experience this new life!

"And he said unto them, Go ye into all the world, and preach the gospel to every creature. He that believeth and is baptized shall be saved; but he that believeth not shall be damned."-Mark 16:15-16

"...whosoever shall call on the name of the Lord shall be saved."-Acts 2:21

If you prayed this prayer or would like to receive more materials to help you grow in your walk with Christ, please write to us at:

Christopher Lynn Ministries P.O. Box 521072 Tulsa, Oklahoma 74152 or visit us online at: www.christopherlynnministries.org **We want to hear from *YOU*!**

Sign up for our *Monthly Newsletter!*

Visit www.clynn.org

Find us on  @christopherlynnministries

Made in the USA
Columbia, SC
26 July 2022

64055824R00076